The MACAT Library
世界思想宝库钥匙丛书

解析托马斯·潘恩

《常识》

AN ANALYSIS OF

THOMAS PAINE'S

COMMON SENSE

Ian Jackson ◎ 著

杨元刚 ◎ 译

上海外语教育出版社
SHANGHAI FOREIGN LANGUAGE EDUCATION PRESS

MACAT

目　录

CONTENTS

引言

要 点

- 托马斯·潘恩 1737 年出生在英格兰，因其撰写诸多时政宣传册激励了北美殖民地反抗大英帝国统治而为世人铭记。
- 《常识》呼吁美利坚独立，并阐释了北美殖民地取得独立的路径。
- 潘恩的这本宣传册阐述的政治思想通俗易懂，市场销量巨大，直接推动了美国独立革命*的爆发，这场军事斗争导致了大英帝国在北美十三个殖民地的独立和美利坚合众国的诞生。

托马斯·潘恩其人

托马斯·潘恩 1737 年出生在英格兰，其父系一名贵格会*教徒。贵格会是基督教的一个分支，反对战争和暴力。其时受教育者不多，且潘恩的家境也不富裕，但他上了文法学校*——我们今天称之为"初中"或"中学"——并就读至十三岁。潘恩在文法学校里接受了拉丁文、希腊文、数学和圣经的基本教育。

潘恩的早期生活并不是很顺畅。他的两次婚姻都不长久，数次创业也均以失败告终。1772 年在英国海关任职时（工作是督查进口货物），潘恩撰写了他的第一部政治宣传册《海关职员的境况》。该书呼吁英国政府给职员提供更好的工作条件，增加薪资。1774 年初他被英国海关部门解聘。

1774 年 9 月，潘恩结识了本杰明·富兰克林*——一名杰出的发明家、作家和政治活动家。富兰克林后来成为美国的开国元勋之一。富兰克林对潘恩印象深刻，他建议潘恩移居北美，并亲自给潘恩写了一封推荐信。

　　为了争夺海外贸易利益，英国和法国之间发生了七年战争（1756—1763）*。潘恩到达费城时，英法七年战争已结束11年，但北美殖民地的政局非常不稳定。英国虽然赢得了战争，却背上了沉重的债务，于是想逼迫北美殖民地承担战争开支。英国对北美殖民地收税，以弥补战争亏空，同时却拒绝给北美居民在英国议会的代表权。潘恩跟当时许多北美殖民地居民一样，对此感到非常愤慨。潘恩认为北美殖民地必须独立，并在《常识》中阐明了他的理由。

《常识》的主要内容

　　潘恩坚信北美殖民地尽管在军事上处于劣势，但终将赢得独立。其时一国最重要的军事力量是海军，而英国拥有世界上最强大的海军。不过，潘恩声称北美殖民地拥有很多英国不具备的优势。比如，北美殖民地自然资源丰富，森林茂盛，这适合制造舰船。此外，英国士兵为了到达北美战场，需要远涉重洋。

　　更重要的是，潘恩认为，英国的统治不得人心。潘恩希望建立一个自由的社会，在这个社会里一切由人民作主，政出民意而非宫廷。《常识》中的观念通俗易懂，时至今日仍然影响着美国政治。正因如此，《常识》一书成了美国历史的一个重要组成部分。

　　《常识》所提出的思想并非潘恩独创，实际上他吸收了欧洲启蒙运动*的思想精华，欧洲知识分子在启蒙运动中重视理性和个性甚于传统。启蒙思想家关注的焦点问题包含着对社会正义的追寻，他们思考如何让社会变得更加公正。然而此前尚无人尝试根据启蒙运动的思想原则建立一个社会。

　　潘恩助力改变了这一切。在赢得独立战争之后，北美殖民地人民根据启蒙运动思想家所倡导的个人自由的原则建立了美利坚合众国。当时还有人相信，这样的社会制度会导致混乱，而美国的成功证明他们是错误的。因其撰写的政论宣传册在政治变革中的作用，潘恩被看成美国的开国元勋之一。

潘恩的研究者出于两个原因看到了《常识》的宝贵价值：首先，《常识》帮助人们了解18世纪北美殖民地居民对政局所怀有的担忧和想法，同时向人们披露了当时有部分人虽然对时局不满意，却仍希望留在大英帝国*的体系中。其次，潘恩的写作风格影响了未来政论文的写作风格。潘恩吸收了精英政治家的思想观念，并用浅显易懂的笔墨表达出来，让识字者皆能读懂。正如政治历史学家埃里克·弗纳*所说：潘恩不仅向广大北美人民，也向全球读者"传播了政府治理新愿景"。[1]

《常识》的学术价值

潘恩在《常识》中列举了赞同北美殖民地独立的理由，抨击了那些企图仍然保留大英帝国子民身份的人。惟其如此，这篇檄文给读者描绘了18世纪大众的感情和心态。因而该书能帮助学生理解北美殖民地的历史和政治，也有助于解释为什么时至今日对很多人来说自由仍然非常重要。

《常识》写作具有创新性，它使深奥的政治思想变得通俗易懂。这些思想不仅贯穿了美国独立战争，还影响了后人，成为日常政治生活的一部分。比如，潘恩的政治理念被写入美国《独立宣言》*和美国宪法*：前者是英属北美十三个殖民地宣告脱离大英帝国的文告；后者确立了美国公民的权利以及政府的性质和义务。这两个文件奠定了美国政体的基础，美国宪法在全世界产生了广泛的影响。

潘恩还普及了过去只有少数受过良好教育的知识精英能够理解的思想。比如，当时许多人认为宗教自由和言论自由是危险的，潘恩则说明并非如此，认为两者会让世界变得更美好。

潘恩的写作风格表明，政论文写作越是通俗易懂，越是为老百姓喜爱。《常识》这本小册子销售数量巨大，没有《常识》的宣传普及，美国独立战争就不会获得如此广泛的支持。而且这种支持还让美国开国元勋在独立战争结束后能将这些新的理念付诸实践。新的美国体制取得了成功，这也促使诸多欧洲人思考效仿。过去人们认为一个自由的国家会导致社会混乱，而美国的实践证明这种观念不堪一击，于是人们开始想从政府手中争取更多的自由和权利。在这个层面上，我们可以看到潘恩的《常识》是如何深刻影响了全世界人民对待政治体制的态度。

---

1. 埃里克·弗纳：《托马斯·潘恩和革命的美国》，伦敦、纽约、牛津：牛津大学出版社，1976年，第 XVI 页。

第一部分：学术渊源

1 作者生平与历史背景

要点 🗝

- 《常识》在激励民众支持北美殖民地独立方面发挥了促进作用。

- 1774 年潘恩移居北美殖民地，在此为自己理念的传播和实践而奔走雄辩。

- 美国革命战争 * 是英属北美十三个殖民地和大英帝国军队之间的军事冲突，最终形成年轻的合众国。战争为创建一个基于启蒙运动 * 思想法则的国家提供了实践机会。启蒙运动是一场宣传理性与个性自由的欧洲文化及思想运动。

为何要读这部著作？

托马斯·潘恩的《常识》于 1776 年首次出版。他在这本宣传册中称，北美殖民地和英国之间的政治经济联系迟早会终结。[1]潘恩批判了英国的世袭君主制 *（王权在同一家族内部代代相传的制度），并断言让一个遥远的小岛国去统治一个新大陆是行不通的。他声称英国让北美殖民地居民遭受了很多经济和社会的不公，这些不公侵犯了北美殖民地居民的个人自由。

尽管很多北美殖民地居民承认英国和北美殖民地之间存在不公和痛苦，有些人还是相信双方可以达成和解。但潘恩反驳说："祈求北美殖民地脱离英国是理所当然、天经地义的事。"[2]他坚持认为独立是最好的抉择。他的观念促使北美殖民地居民的态度明显转变，大量民众开始支持美国独立革命。但应该注意到，《常识》出版的主要目的是政治宣传，也就是说，该书的写作不是为了给百姓提供不偏不倚的信息，而是说服当时的读者接受潘恩的思想。

《常识》概述了 18 世纪的政治思潮，帮助普及那个时代的政治思想。此外，《常识》能帮助我们理解美国独立革命取得胜利的原因，因为美国独立革命在某种程度上影响了西方的政治体制，这种影响至今还在持续。

> "祈求北美殖民地脱离英国是理所当然、天经地义的事。"
>
> —— 托马斯·潘恩：《常识》

作者生平

1737 年，潘恩出生于英格兰，其父是一名贵格会 * 成员，其母是一名英国国教徒。他的早年生活不为人知。他在一所文法学校 * 读到十三岁并接受了基本教育。他的第一场婚姻结局很凄惨，妻子和女儿均死于难产。他与第二任妻子伊丽莎白·奥利弗之间的婚姻仅维持了四年，于 1774 年正式分居。潘恩多次创业，比如连经营一家烟草店最后也以失败而告终。

潘恩在伦敦担任海关职员时第一次尝试写作，《海关职员的境况》是一本仅有 21 页的小宣传册，他在该书中呼吁给海关职员提供更好的工作条件并增加薪酬。该书出版不久他就遭到解雇。

1774 年 9 月，潘恩被引荐给美国政治理论家、科学家本杰明·富兰克林 *，于是他的生活发生了改变。我们现在对这次会晤知之甚少，但是两人见面后不久，潘恩决定启程赴北美费城。1774 年 11 月 30 日，潘恩到达费城，不久他就成为北美殖民地的一名公民。富兰克林给潘恩写了一封推荐信，这在当时是一份很重要的担保。1775 年 1 月，潘恩受聘担任一家期刊《费城杂志》的编辑。他在此投身于北美政治，逐渐形成了自己的独特风格。

创作背景

　　1774 年潘恩到达北美时，北美还是大英帝国的一块主权领土，不过形势岌岌可危。为了争夺对美洲殖民地的控制，英法之间爆发了七年战争 *。虽然英国赢得了这场战争，但是也付出了沉重的代价。因此英国政府通过征税将这次战争费用转嫁到北美殖民地身上，但征税的议案未经殖民地人民同意，而且北美人民纳税后，英国政府拒绝给予他们在英国议会中的代表权，这引起了北美当地居民的不满。

　　1773 年波士顿倾茶事件 * 发生后，北美殖民地的政治形势持续恶化。殖民地人民登上了停泊在波士顿港的三艘英国货船，将托运的茶叶倒入海中。作为回应，英国国会一连颁布了五部法律，统称《强制法案》³，制定这些法律是为了惩戒北美殖民地的反抗，重建英国对北美殖民地的控制。马萨诸塞州反抗最为强烈，故首当其冲。比如，《强制法案》关闭了北美商贸中心波士顿港，将马萨诸塞州政府的控制权交给英国政府任命的总督，总督有权规定，受到控告的马萨诸塞州政府官员必须送到英国进行审判，而且总督可以在无人占据的房屋中屯驻军队。

　　果不其然，新颁布的《强制法案》激起了北美殖民地民众的愤慨，他们将该法令称为"不可容忍法案" *。结果，北美殖民地召集了第一届大陆会议 *，北美十三州中的十二个州派代表参会（佐治亚州未派代表参会），代表们于 1774 年 9 月至 10 月在费城开会。这差不多刚好是潘恩抵达费城的时间。

大陆会议向英国国王乔治三世*发出请愿，要求他消弭民众对《强制法案》的愤慨，并处理其他各类争端。然而该请愿被英国拒绝，于是北美殖民地于 1775 年 5 月召开了第二届大陆会议*，决定做好与英国进行军事斗争的准备。当时大部分北美居民认为这场战争不可避免，虽然不是所有人都同意这个观点。

1775 年 4 月 19 日，在波士顿附近的莱克星顿和康科德*，北美殖民地打响了反抗英国的枪声，揭开了美国独立战争的序幕。1776 年 7 月 4 日，第二届大陆会议发表《独立宣言》*，宣布北美十三州脱离英国而独立。

---

1. 托马斯·潘恩：《常识》，纽约：多弗尔出版公司，1997 年，第 22 页。
2. 潘恩：《常识》，第 22 页。
3. 五部《强制法令》中只有四部是直接针对北美十三个殖民地的反抗所做的回应，第五部与魁北克边界有关。

2 学术背景

要点 🔑

- 《常识》一书探讨了北美殖民地出现的政治危机，分析了民众面对危机所应采取的行动。

- 启蒙运动是当时欧洲思想界的主流思潮，日益强调理性和个性，主张个体的权利高于国家的权力。

- 潘恩是自学成才的，没有受过正式的政治哲学教育。

著作语境

18世纪北美殖民地人民存在一种民族自豪感，潘恩的《常识》一书即代表了对这一感情的诉求。尽管他的作品反映了"同时代启蒙思想家所达成的共识"[1]，但他的目标不是教育民众，而是激发政治变革。他的著作是为了帮助北美殖民地的普通居民领会他的观念，他把直白的论辩和圣经典故结合起来，并利用了殖民地居民对当时政治环境的感受。

潘恩没有提及英国思想家洛克*、日内瓦政治哲学家卢梭*、法国政治哲学家和作家伏尔泰*等18世纪启蒙思想家，也没提及潘恩圈子中更接近的其他思想家，比如美国政治理论家和科学家本杰明·富兰克林*。考虑到这些启蒙运动的巨匠对18世纪思想的贡献，潘恩显然受到了他们的影响。

洛克通常被认为是现代自由主义*思想之父，他和伏尔泰一道为个人权利和政教分离而辩护。卢梭有关社会不公和政治制度方面的论述对美国独立革命*和法国大革命*都产生了影响。年轻的美利坚合众国在独立革命中义无反顾地脱离大英帝国而独立，法国公民在大革命中揭竿而起，扭转了政治秩序，推翻了君主体制，建立了共和国。

在 18 世纪，普通民众还不熟悉有关个人权利和自由的思想。北美殖民地还臣服于英国国王的统治，尽管英国国王不再拥有绝对的王权，但北美殖民地居民言论和行动上仍然受到许多限制。与当下不同，当时北美民众并没有什么可替代现有政府体制的选项可供尝试。严格地说，那些赞同个性自由的人们很难去回应那些认为个性自由会导致无政府状态 * 的人们。

> "有人问，美洲的国王在哪里？朋友，我将告诉你，他居高统治国家，但不会像大不列颠王室的畜生一样，在人间制造混乱。"
>
> —— 潘恩:《常识》

学科概览

当时的思想氛围非常不稳定，因为启蒙思想家正在挑战已有的宗教观、政体观和个人权利观。像伏尔泰一样，潘恩也是个自然神论 * 信奉者。他认为，人们对上帝的信仰应该是建立在理性基础之上，而非在传统基础之上。同样他还认为政府也应如此。尽管潘恩在《常识》中明白无误地阐述了这些论断，但是人们仍然可以看到启蒙思想家对这本小册子的潜在涵义的影响。

《常识》中的一个核心观念就是社会契约论 *，这也是启蒙政治思想的核心理念。社会契约论的思想是英国哲学家托马斯·霍布斯 * 创立的，他认为人性由理性主导，同时为了建立良好的政体，公民同意让渡部分个体权利给政府，但是这些权利的数量应有一个限度。霍布斯认为人类会生活在社会混乱之中，除非他们受到如君主制一样强大而具有威权的政府统治。

潘恩赞同霍布斯的观点，同意公民社会需要建立某种形式的政府。但是潘恩强烈反对公民让渡很多个人权利。潘恩辩解说，作为个体的人不仅是自由的、平等的、独立的，而且他们唯一的国王就是上帝，上帝高高在上统治人间，"不会像大不列颠王室的畜生一样，在人间制造混乱"。[2]

约翰·洛克对潘恩的思想影响也很大。洛克也相信人性由理性主宰，他主张人们应当自愿放弃个体的部分自由，以便建立一个公民社会和某种形式的政府。洛克不赞同霍布斯的观点，他认为人民应该放弃较少的权利，而潘恩在这一点上比洛克走得更远。在潘恩看来，公民应该尽可能少放弃个人权利，因为有些权利是无法放弃的，哪怕自愿也不行。

虽然潘恩认识到公民社会需要领袖，但他希望建立总统制*。在总统制中，领导人由人民选举产生，而不是像君主制那样世袭继承而来。在世袭君主制*中，权力在一个家族内部流转，一代传给一代。此外潘恩还认为总统任期应是短期的，权力应受限制。[3]在《常识》中，潘恩主张他的思想必须付诸实践。这本宣传册的内容已超出了哲学争论。

学术渊源

尽管我们今天已经看到启蒙思想影响了潘恩，但我们还可更仔细地审视他的原则。潘恩信奉自由主义，这是一种强调自由、平等和定期举行竞选的政治哲学。他还受到共和主义*的影响，共和主义否认国家首脑是一个世袭职位的观念，拒绝接受国王或君主世袭的统治原则。最后，潘恩还是一名激进主义*者，当时这个称呼是指那些希望北美殖民地脱离英国以便建立一个更加公正的社会的人。今天我们应当注意到，激进主义逐渐指代任何形式的极端意识形态。潘恩也可能从本杰明·富兰克林那里学到了很多，后者是一名具有巨大影响力的政治家和博学之士*（指一个人的学识横跨几个不同的领域）。

与潘恩同时代的启蒙运动精英一直在为如何最理想地建设社会而努力。霍布斯甚至认为，如果没有一个强有力的统治者，社会中的强者会统治或奴役弱者，因此他认为生命权是人民拥有的唯一不可被剥夺的（必须受保障的）权利。洛克的思想没有那么极端，他认为人民拥有广泛的不可争议的权利，但是为了和平与安全，他们仍需让渡出部分权利。

然而在潘恩看来，霍布斯心目中的君主是一个暴君，而洛克倡导的君主立宪制*中，虽然君王的权力受到宪法的制约，却比暴君好不了多少。潘恩把这些思想和当时的思考结合起来，比如他吸收了卢梭的思想，卢梭赞同民主政治。虽然这些思想今天看起来并不激进，但是却和当时的普遍观念相抵牾。

1. 克莱格·纳尔逊：《托马斯·潘恩：他的生平、他的时代和现代国家的诞生》，伦敦：概览书局，2007 年，第 8 页。
2. 托马斯·潘恩：《常识》，纽约：多弗尔出版公司，1997 年，第 31 页。
3. 托马斯·潘恩：《常识》，第 30 页。

3 主导命题

要点 🗝

- 潘恩希望保障个体权利高于一切。

- 在当时大多数欧洲国家，个体权利不如对国王和国家的忠诚重要。

- 潘恩让每个人理解有关个体权利的辩论。

核心问题

托马斯·潘恩的《常识》试图回答两个问题：第一，脱离英国独立是北美殖民地人民心之所向吗？第二，北美殖民地脱离英国独立可以实现吗？

潘恩写作这本小册子就是为了宣传上述思想。他认为上述两个问题的答案是肯定的，并没有尝试做出不偏不倚的探讨。美国独立革命*爆发后不久，他就开始写作《常识》。当时很多人，包括大陆会议的一些代表，仍然期盼与英国和解。正因为此，这些核心问题极为重要：潘恩的主要目的是让北美殖民地民众和领袖们明白，独立是正确的选择。

潘恩称英国的统治就是暴政。他对北美殖民地能否独立没有很大的把握。在那个时代，北美殖民地人民的反抗极有可能失败。根据我们现在了解的信息，人们很容易忽视潘恩的论点是一场多么大的豪赌。这场豪赌最终获得成功，这是让《常识》流芳百世的令人信服的原因之一。

> "就像在专制统治中国王就是法律一样，在自由的国家中法律就是国王。"
>
> —— 托马斯·潘恩:《常识》

参与者

尽管《常识》没有援引具体的政治或哲学理论，但是潘恩的思想脉络很明显。在这本小册子中，我们发现潘恩受到了一位重要思想家——英国哲学家洛克——的影响。

洛克有关文明社会的概念建立在公民的自然权利*和社会契约论*基础之上，前者认为所有公民的自然权利应受保障，后者则认为个体的某些自由必须让渡，以确保社会的和平公正。

潘恩接受了洛克的观点，认为只有经过公民同意，一个人才能获得永久社会成员的资格，并刻意用煽动性语言表述了这个观点。[1]比如，潘恩在《常识》中写道：独立绝不仅仅意味着"我们是否将制定自己的法律，或者是否像北美大陆的敌人——英国国王——所教导我们的那样，'世界上除了君言别无他法。'"。[2]当时发表的大多数启蒙运动*作品都不像潘恩的文字那么具有煽动性，因为这些作品的阅读对象是知识分子，而这些作者害怕被逮捕，因而措辞谨慎。

不是每一位启蒙运动思想家都相信同一个版本的社会契约论，潘恩从各个流派的学说中吸收了不同的思想营养。潘恩还受到另外一位哲学家卢梭的影响。让-雅克·卢梭出生于日内瓦（现在是瑞士联邦的一座城市）。他在《社会契约论》中称，为了维护社会的集体利益，公民必须遵守法律，这一点很重要。[3]跟卢梭一样，潘恩相信法律建立在理性基础之上的重要性。他在《常识》中写道："就像在专制统治中国王就是法律一样，在自由的国家中法律就是国王。"[4]

潘恩与卢梭的区别在于，他看重个人权利，认为个人权利重于集体利益。他摒弃了北美殖民地居民应该放弃什么权利的问题，因为他认为英国法律是不正当的。"如果你反对独立的话，你就不知道自己能干什么。"潘恩在书中写道："如果你让治理缺位，你将为永恒暴政打开大门。"[5]

在作出上述论断的时候，他把自己偏激的思想表达得更加激进化*。潘恩的《常识》抨击了英国的统治，该书质疑公民应该把什么权利让渡给统治者，并且最重要的是，什么人才有权统治。

同期争议

潘恩 1776 年出版《常识》时，思想界风雷激荡，百家争鸣，当时有启蒙运动思想、传统君主制思想和现实政治*思想（只关注实际利益而非道德考量）。潘恩采纳众家观点，经常吸收激进的思想并把它们推向极端。

例如，洛克认为君主的权力应受宪法的制约。潘恩发展了这个观念，他嘲笑君主立宪制*概念："为什么英国宪法令人作呕，难道不是因为君主立宪制已经毒害了共和体制，难道不是因为王冠已经垄断了下议院？"[6]法国思想家伏尔泰*也同样相信英国比法国自由，因为英国建立了君主立宪制。然而潘恩公开摒弃了这种观念，认为英式自由徒有虚名。

即使是北美独立革命的支持者，如政治家约翰·亚当斯*（后来成为美国第二任总统）等，都认为《常识》中的思想太激进，在亚当斯看来，潘恩倾向于使用错误的二元对立观，认为现实社会只有非白即黑的两种选择，而实际上存在多种可能性。在其著作《政府论》（1776 年）中，亚当斯驳斥了潘恩有关国家可以由一个单独的立法机构治理的观点。亚当斯认为："人民不可能长期自由，也不可能永久幸福，如果他们的政府只存在于一个立法机构中。"[7]

为了在当今时代理解《常识》的思想内容，读者应该对 18 世纪欧洲启蒙思想有所涉猎。我们应该记住，潘恩从启蒙思想家那里借鉴了很多思想观念，他花了时间去追寻这些思想的来龙去脉，目的是希望自己的宣传册简洁易懂。

最后，潘恩的观念通常要比他学习借鉴的同代人著作中的观念更加极端，一个原因就是该书创作的时代环境。欧洲的学术著作能经得起抽象的辩论，而潘恩的思想却必须马上运用于北美殖民地风云变化的政治环境，民众几乎没有时间就其观念展开论辩。

1. 约翰·洛克：《政府论》，彼得·拉斯莱特编，剑桥：剑桥大学出版社，1988 年，第 111 页。
2. 托马斯·潘恩：《常识》，纽约：多弗尔出版公司，1997 年，第 27 页。
3. 克里斯托弗·D. 莱特：《卢梭社会契约论导读》，纽约：康特农出版社，2008 年，第 33 页。
4. 托马斯·潘恩：《常识》，第 31—32 页。
5. 托马斯·潘恩：《常识》，第 33 页。
6. 托马斯·潘恩：《常识》，第 17 页。
7. 约翰·亚当斯：《政府论》，http://www.constitution.org/jadams/thoughts.htm，2013 年 11 月 7 日查阅。

4 作者贡献

要点 🔑

- 潘恩认为政府应该只为人民的意愿这一唯一利益服务。

- 潘恩把启蒙运动的思想付诸实践，对美国的形成做出了巨大的贡献。

- 潘恩懂得为了推动政治变革，他必须把抽象的哲学理念转化成实用理念。

作者目标

在《常识》的写作过程中，托马斯·潘恩很清楚他的目标读者的局限性。《常识》所吸收的思想观念对 1776 年北美殖民地的普通读者来说还不熟悉，也不容易解释。故此潘恩的著作不是一本哲学作品，而是对采取行动的号召。《常识》写得思路清晰，文笔简洁，避免使用复杂的暗喻和深奥的论辩来说理。

在 18 世纪的新英格兰地区，能读书识字的民众还不是很普遍，而且对宣传册的篇幅长度也有限制。《常识》的写作目的就是为了供人们在公共聚会上大声朗读，如果写得太长，读者很难做到这一点。这也是这本小册子被看成是革命读物的一个原因：该书语言平实，言简意赅，让普通民众得以理解复杂的哲学思想和政治观念。

《常识》被称为"美国第一本自救手册"，尤其是对"那些缺少了国王就无法想象生活是什么样子的北美居民"而言。[1]《常识》出版后立刻成了畅销读物[2]，引起了新大陆人民的广泛热议。尤其重要的是，《常识》还激励了乔治·华盛顿率领的美洲大陆民兵的士气。华盛顿后来成为年轻的合众国的第一任总统。

> "潘恩的作品在美洲和欧洲都产生了巨大的影响，其原因未能得到充分的解释。潘恩与北美民众广泛参与政治活动——从而成为革命年代的主要成就——的关系还未明晰。"
>
> ——埃里克·弗纳：《潘恩与革命的美洲》

研究方法

潘恩驳斥了北美殖民地与大不列颠和解的可能性，尽管有人希望如此。潘恩对那些反对北美殖民地独立的人的回应，有两点值得注意。

第一，他汲取了启蒙思想家的观点，认为政治制度应该建立在理性基础之上，而不是传统基础之上。其次，潘恩非常了解当时的北美政治，且能把启蒙思想明确地运用到其中。潘恩的创新在于没有去追问北美殖民地是否应该独立，而是追问应该如何获得独立。他认为留在英国的统治体系内根本不值得考虑。

当时大多数政治哲学家会假设一些例证以说明其思想行之有效，潘恩却能利用引起民众群起抗议的真实事件来说理。比如说，英国政府为了应对马萨诸塞州的倾茶事件而颁布的《强制法案》，以之惩罚北美殖民地居民的叛逆行为（或曰反叛行为）。潘恩的思想不是抽象的说教，而是能够应用于当时的时政事件。

当欧洲思想家在问人民应该拥有什么权利的时候，潘恩却指出了人民有哪些权利已经被剥夺或被滥用。潘恩的《常识》将理性分析和情感煽动结合起来，引起了新大陆读者的共鸣。

时代贡献

潘恩继承了日内瓦派启蒙哲学家让-雅克·卢梭等诸多人物的思想。潘恩"非常尊敬卢梭"。[3] 卢梭主张民主是最好的政治体制；他仔细研究了英国哲学家约翰·洛克*和托马斯·霍布斯*的思想，提出了天赋人权说。历史学家克里斯托弗·希金斯指出，"虽然我们还不知道潘恩是否读过霍布斯的作品，而且潘恩一直否认他读过洛克的《政府论》"，[4] 但是我们仍可以发现霍布斯和洛克对《常识》的影响。

潘恩善于直接运用上述哲学家的思想去分析当时北美殖民地的困境。借此，他不仅批评了英国的暴政，还批评了英国的政治体制。与洛克和霍布斯不同，潘恩拒绝接受国王的统治，哪怕国王的权力受到宪法的制约也不行。相反，他选择这样一种体制，该体制要求领导者通过选举产生并定期更换。

后人很难确定潘恩在学术思想界的位置。他在《常识》中采取反对君主立宪制的立场，这让我们把他看成一位共和主义者*；然而他又强调平等、自由和个人的权利，这又表明他是一名自由主义者*乃至激进主义者。然而，我们只有通过仔细阅读潘恩后期的作品，比如《人权论》*（1791年），才能明确地说他受到了社会契约论*的影响。在《人权论》中，潘恩采用当时的政治理论来解释政治事件，如北美社会危机的形成和法国大革命*的产生。更重要的是，他吸纳综合了那些符合自己自由观的不同来源的思想。

1. 克莱格·纳尔逊:《托马斯·潘恩:他的生平、时代和现代国家的诞生》,伦敦:概览书局,2007 年,第 84 页。

2. 托马斯·潘恩:《托马斯·潘恩读本》,麦克·福特、伊萨克·克兰姆尼编,伦敦:企鹅书屋,1987 年,第 10 页。

3. 克里斯托弗·希金斯:《托马斯·潘恩的人权论》,纽约:格罗夫出版社,2006 年,第 95 页。

4. 克里斯托弗·希金斯:《托马斯·潘恩的人权论》,第 106 页。

第二部分：学术思想

5 思想主脉

要点 🔑

- 《常识》认为英国背弃了北美殖民地，从道义上说，北美民众必须为独立而战。
- 潘恩表明北美民众对英国的痛恨代表着社会存在较大的不公。
- 他采用直白的、戏剧化的写作风格，使用读者熟悉的语言说服读者。

核心主题

潘恩《常识》的论点前提是"最好状态的政府也只是一种必须忍受的罪恶"[1]，而最坏状态的政府却是一种"无法忍受的罪恶"。严格地说，潘恩在《常识》的开篇便描述各类政体，尤其是君主制的有害性。他认为北美独立无法避免。他坚持认为若没有独立，英国的暴政会继续引起社会不公。他把这些观点串联起来，提及一个对启蒙运动*思想家来说非常重要的哲学概念——自然状态*的审视，即假设社会形成之前人们的生活状态。

潘恩对社会契约论*的解释非常细致，社会契约论设想人类天性受理性制约，为了建立稳定的政府，人民才必须出让很多的个人权利。

首先，他请读者想象每个人自己在"自然状态"下的生活。在潘恩看来，既然"一个人的力量远远无法满足他个体的需求，他的思想也和他个体永恒的孤独远远不相匹配"[2]，那么人们想创立一个"社会"[3]就成为顺理成章的事了。为了团结起来，民众不得不协商达成共同规则，并选择领导人去治理社会。

但潘恩在书中写到，政府孕育于"黑暗和盲从时代"[4]，业已"不完美，受到社会动荡的影响，无法兑现它对民众的承诺"[5]。在潘恩看来，这些"缺陷"样本包括英国的不成文宪法和世袭君主制*——之所以称为"不成文宪法"，是因为英国的宪法存在于各种各样的文书和司法实践中，没有形成一部单独的统一的文本。英国世袭君主制规定国王的权力按照传统一代传给一代。潘恩尤其把国王看成是各种社会不公的来源。

潘恩谴责英国政府那些年的罪孽，不仅包含对北美殖民地收取苛捐杂税却剥夺他们在议会中的代表权，还包含1775年莱克星顿、康科德*和邦克山的血腥战役——当时北美民兵在马萨诸塞州抗击英国军队，伤亡惨重。

在潘恩看来，和解不会解决北美殖民地居民的痛苦，因为和解不会改变殖民地仍由英国国王统治的事实。严格地说，潘恩控告那些支持和解的人是"为永恒暴政打开大门"[6]。因为英国政府已拒绝同意北美殖民地的要求，潘恩认为剩下的选择只有两个：要么投降，要么革命。从这个角度看，战争似乎不可避免：北美殖民地居民的处境是无法忍受的，也不会有任何改变，除非他们脱离英国统治。

> "每一种状态下的社会都是一个福音，但是最好状态的政府也只是一种必须忍受的罪恶，最坏状态的政府是一种无法忍受的罪恶。"
>
> ——托马斯·潘恩：《常识》

思想探究

潘恩反对的不仅是英国政府的政策。他在《常识》中写到，英国的政制是腐败的。他抨击英国的世袭君主制是"对繁荣昌盛的羞辱和侵扰"[7]，辩论说这个问题的解决思路就是改变该制度。在潘恩看来，这就是北美人民必须独立的原因：因为英国没有意愿去改变君主立宪制*，他们认为这是一个自由的运转有效的体制。

北美必须脱离英国母体而独立。潘恩认为欧洲旧世界"充满压迫"，自由"在全世界受到追击"[8]。潘恩认为和英国的谈判绝对不会改变现状。因此，北美人民有必要根据启蒙思想家们的政治理念建立一种新的政治体制，至少把启蒙先贤们的部分理念付诸实践，（比如托马斯·霍布斯*，约翰·洛克*，让-雅克·卢梭*，以及荷兰哲学家胡果·格劳秀斯*——他是 17 世纪最早介绍自然人权利的思想家）

在请求读者思考人类在自然状态下是一种什么生活样态之时，潘恩还请读者重新评估一下他们所赖以成长的社会规范。潘恩声称他是从"自然法则"[9]中推导出政府形式。他还辩解说，自然状态证明世袭君主制是不合逻辑的——或者用他自己的话说就是，世袭君主制"是人类画虎得犬的行为，反而变成了一个笑谈"[10]。而且潘恩坚持认为，"那些以为自己生而为王，有权去统治别人的人，会很快变得傲慢无礼"。对潘恩而言，这个逻辑非常清晰：自然界没有君王，所以"人类社会也不应该有君王"[11]。

语言表述

《常识》的核心思想最好被理解为一系列的论辩和反驳，设计这些论辩是为了激励读者支持北美独立革命。潘恩在书中开篇就否定了政府不是为人民利益服务的错误观念。他特别批判了世袭君主制，因为它在很多方面限制了个体权利。潘恩引用了很多例证来说明《圣经》没有赞同国王的观念，他对大英帝国的统治进行了全力抨击，嘲笑英国这么一个岛国居然统治一个新大陆，更别说它还统治世界上很多地区，这真是荒谬无比。

潘恩心平气和有条有理地支持人权，或者说人权应该受到保障的观念，这种冷静和逻辑抑制了他对旧制度的愤慨。潘恩一方面证明英国统治的不公，另一方面强调北美独立战争的经济可行性。潘恩的论点既回应了北美殖民地人民的具体关切，又表达了其时人们日益增长的愤慨。

潘恩用戏剧化的、富有感情的、具有煽动性的英语写作《常识》一书。他希望当时的读者容易理解北美殖民地为什么要为独立而战。这本小册子今天读起来不易理解，那是因为它写于250年前：潘恩不是为后人而写此书，现代读者可能不太熟悉他那个时代的政治事件。不过对于政府到底应该拥有多少权力以统治个体，潘恩在书中所作的论辩时至今日对读者仍具有参考意义。

---

1. 托马斯·潘恩，《常识》，纽约：多弗尔出版公司，1997年，第3页。
2. 托马斯·潘恩，《常识》，第3页。
3. 托马斯·潘恩，《常识》，第3页。
4. 托马斯·潘恩，《常识》，第5页。
5. 托马斯·潘恩，《常识》，第5页。

6. 托马斯·潘恩,《常识》, 第 32 页。

7. 托马斯·潘恩,《常识》, 第 12 页。

8. 托马斯·潘恩,《常识》, 第 33 页。

9. 托马斯·潘恩,《常识》, 第 5 页。

10. 托马斯·潘恩,《常识》, 第 12 页。

11. 托马斯·潘恩,《常识》, 第 33 页。

6 思想支脉

要点 🗝

- 《常识》提出北美殖民地可以打赢独立战争并从中获益。
- 潘恩的论辩令北美民众质疑他们对英国国王的忠诚。
- 并非所有潘恩在《常识》中提出的要求都是现实的。

其他思想

尽管潘恩《常识》中的主要目标是说服北美殖民地居民相信北美独立是最好的行动抉择，他还在书中讨论了其他重要问题。他清楚地讲述了大英帝国统治所犯下的罪行，讨论了北美殖民地当前的现状——尤其是他们的军事力量。

读者应该意识到，潘恩不是在编写一部教材，他没有必要去提供细节或证据。比如，当谈到"莱克星顿大屠杀"时，他没有解释说这是指当英国军队试图摧毁北美民兵的军事补给仓库的时候[1]，北美民兵在马萨诸塞州的莱克星顿镇和康科德镇*开始的抗英战斗。同样，潘恩写道，"几千人被英国野蛮军队剥夺了生命"[2]，他没有具体写是哪些冲突。

潘恩明白，和英国的开战将花费很多财力，并且风险很大。他注意到北美殖民地没有债务负担，因此准备好"抗击全世界的力量"[3]。他还说既然北美拥有"世界上人数最多且训练有素的武装民兵"[4]，北美殖民地不可能由于经济实力的原因，在挑战英国的统治方面畏首畏尾。英国优势在于海军，潘恩承认其"令人生畏"，但他对此不屑一顾，因为"只有不到十分之一的英国海军力量可以随时投入战斗"[5]。尽管北美殖民地没有自己的军舰，潘恩坚信没有哪个国家"能像北美一样，地理条件这么优越，能够仅凭内部力量就可以组建一支舰队"[6]。

这些想法是推测性的，而且有点夸大事实。英国海军确实有点混乱，但是要说北美能够组建一支舰队并能与英国抗衡，那确实是有点荒谬。读者应该意识到，英国与殖民地之间的战争主要在陆地进行，所以潘恩声称北美能够组建一支舰队最终驱逐英国海军，其实无关紧要。

> "通过这种生动的语言，潘恩传播了一种乌托邦式的新愿景——建立一个人人平等的社会，他这样传播有关天赋人权与共和主义思想，很容易让普通民众接受理解。"
>
> ——埃里克·弗纳：《汤姆·潘恩与革命的北美》

思想探究

尽管北美独立革命的成功证明潘恩坚持认为北美居民"不需要畏惧外部敌人"[7]的观点是正确的，但他的有些论断值得怀疑。潘恩有时候更加关注使用戏剧化煽动性的语言鼓动北美居民支持独立战争，而不是作出合理的解释。

比如说，潘恩对北美殖民地军事实力的分析只能解释为他不懂军事，草率而盲目自信，或者说是一种彻底的谎言。虽说英国海军无法封锁北美的全部海岸线，英国军队的报复性攻击确实让人愤慨，比如英军烧毁马萨诸塞州的法尔茅斯*，但是现实情况是1776年北美海军根本不存在。[8]事实上，直到1778年法国、西班牙和荷兰代表美国参战，英国海军的优势才受到挑战。

潘恩在《常识》中引述了作为英国暴政证据的事件，但他避免进行具体描述，比如说莱克星顿战役和康科德战役*。相反，他使用一些抽象空泛的论断去批评英国。例如，英国的宪法不是一个独立的文本，而是包含一系列文件和政策，他说英国的宪法只适合"黑暗和盲从的时代"[9]，英王乔治三世*是"法国杂种"[10]的后代。更重要的是，英国给北美殖民地造成了很多无法饶恕的伤害。

被忽视之处

在《常识》的结尾，潘恩集中探讨了贵格会*。他这样做有两个原因：第一，其父是一名贵格会信徒（尽管其母不是），和贵格会的这层关系让他能够洞察这个群体的意见。其次，更为重要的是，潘恩在费城生活和写作，费城有很多贵格会成员，所以争取他们的支持合乎逻辑。潘恩没有预计到《常识》出版后这么受读者欢迎。

在小册子的这个部分，潘恩采取了一种外交辞令，他反复说明"我们的计划是追求永久和平，我们已经厌倦和英国的纷争，除非北美独立，我们看不到这场纷争何时结束"[11]。

潘恩知道贵格会的宗教信念是和平主义*，他们反对暴力和战争。虽然贵格会成员最初支持抵制英国，比如，他们曾经反对英国国王在北美殖民地的征税政策，但是他们还是对双方日益升级的暴力冲突感到惊骇。诸如波士顿倾茶事件*和《强制法案》*获得英国国会通过等都表明独立战争不可避免。前者是北美殖民地居民的一次政治抗议，当时示威者将一船茶叶倒入波士顿港，以抗议英国政府对北美殖民地收税，却不给北美殖民地在英国议会中的代表权；后者是英国政府对北美反抗所实施的报复性法案。潘恩认为贵格会信徒不会支持殖民地对英战争，这就是潘恩为什么直接与他们探讨这些问题，因为他相信尽管贵格会信徒不会拿起武器，但并不意味着他们必须保持中立。

1. 托马斯·潘恩：《常识》，纽约：多弗尔出版公司，1997年，第26页。

2. 托马斯·潘恩：《常识》，第26页。

3. 托马斯·潘恩：《常识》，第34页。

4. 托马斯·潘恩：《常识》，第34页。

5. 托马斯·潘恩：《常识》，第38页。

6. 托马斯·潘恩：《常识》，第36页。

7. 托马斯·潘恩：《常识》，第39页。

8. 史蒂夫·霍华斯：《走向闪亮的大海：美国海军史1775—1998》，罗曼：俄克拉荷马大学出版社，1991年，第6页。

9. 托马斯·潘恩：《常识》，第5页。

10. 托马斯·潘恩：《常识》，第33页。

11. 托马斯·潘恩：《常识》，第53页。

7 历史成就

要点 ⚷━

- 潘恩的宣传小册子说服了很多北美殖民地居民支持独立。
- 写作《常识》的目的是煽动公众舆情。
- 潘恩在帮助北美实现独立起的作用远大于对美国国家形成的作用。

观点评价

显然，潘恩希望通过《常识》鼓动北美民众支持独立并为之而战。严格地说，潘恩从头至尾保持着一种愤慨的煽动性的语气在写作。此外，他还运用了两个适应面很大的策略去游说读者。首先，潘恩运用了经济的、道德的和神学的证据去证明他的立场。其次，他使用了同样的证据去驳斥反对独立的观点。

我们不清楚潘恩希望对美国独立战争*之后的事件有多大影响。《常识》并没有就如何建立政体提供一个全面而连贯的计划。潘恩确实就政府官员的任期和总统选举等问题提出了一些具体的施政建议。我们不清楚这些想法是否是他政治蓝图中的一部分，或者他是否只是想告诉北美殖民地民众，除了君主世袭制*还有其他的政体选择。

潘恩终究没有直接对美国政府的创立作出贡献。然而当北美殖民地赢得独立后，他实现了他的主要目标。潘恩声称北美殖民地最终将获得独立战争胜利的预判令他似乎成了先知。

> "我们有能力重建一个崭新的世界。"
>
> —— 托马斯·潘恩:《常识》

当时的成就

《常识》的成功必须和美国独立战争的胜利联系起来讨论。更重要的是，《常识》的写作和构思都是根据潘恩的设想，即如何说服普通殖民地民众展开的。我们还应注意到，潘恩的小册子内容直接和北美殖民地的危机联系起来，如果换了不同的时代环境，这本书就不可能出版。

潘恩的名声因为殖民地的胜利而得以延续。他成功地鼓动了北美民众支持独立革命，但并没有停止宣传他的思想。尽管书中探讨北美特定的形势，但他相信他的视野是全球性的，他辩解说美国有能力"重建一个崭新的世界"[1]。实际上，他所助力鼓动的美国独立革命是一个重大的历史事件，比如，这场独立革命后来也影响了不久以后于 1789 年爆发的法国大革命 *。

潘恩的宣传册也引起了学者特别是神学研究专家的兴趣。比如，《常识》抨击了君权神授的观点。在法国，对世袭君主制的抨击直接导致了 1793 年法国国王路易十六 * 被处死。同样，政教分离奠定了新的美国政府创立的基础，后来这种思想也在西方世界产生了重要影响。

《常识》也是美国政治文献的奠基作之一，潘恩慷慨激昂的写作风格确立了美国独立战争的基调，也为美国未来的政治作家树立了榜样。在后期宣传册的写作中，潘恩继续使用这种文笔，比如《美国危机》也沿用了这种风格。他"意识到他正在创立一种新的写作风格"[2]，而"18 世纪大多数作者相信，为平民百姓写作意味着他们必须为了粗糙和琐碎而放弃润饰和精致"[3]。《常识》的成功表明这种观念是错误的。

局限性

潘恩的同时代人，如美国第二任总统约翰·亚当斯*等，对"历史将把美国独立革命归功于托马斯·潘恩"[4]的说法表示愤慨。他们认为美国独立革命更多地受到了政治活动家约瑟夫·休斯*的影响。休斯是美国《独立宣言》*的重要签署人。但是，《常识》仍然应该被看成是一部具有重大影响的著作，是因为该书不仅影响了当时的政治变革，还影响了政论文写作风格。

随着时间的流逝，《常识》中的思想四处传播。潘恩的思想被写进了《独立宣言》和美国宪法*，美国作为一个独立自由国家的历史就是建立在这两部文献之上。更重要的是，潘恩的思想经受了独立战争的考验，不仅是因为启蒙运动*的思想原则被世人广泛接受，而且是因为潘恩的写作风格非常受人欢迎。

1776年《常识》出版之前，政论文写作主要针对知识分子精英阶层。潘恩的写作风格改变了这个传统。根据弗吉尼亚大学历史系教授索菲亚·罗森菲尔德*的研究，"《常识》作为一种政治武器的影响力，可以通过很多反对派的效仿者来衡量，他们抓住了这种形式的商业和宣传效能"[5]。也就是说，我们看到潘恩的写作风格是有影响力的，因为很多模仿者把这种写作风格看成是与公众交流的有效工具。潘恩的写作风格变成了"一种为了未来的政治而激烈论战的常见工具"[6]，因为政治家们明白，一种信息所赖以表达的语言和这条信息本身一样重要，甚至语言形式比内容更重要。

潘恩开创了政论文写作的新传统。正如澳大利亚政治理论研究家约翰·孔乐*指出的那样，民主革命需要"事前进行一场散文写作的民主革命"[7]。潘恩所使用的平实语言后来又在政治演说中得到运用，并取得了良好的效果，如 1933 年至 1945 年任美国总统的富兰克林·罗斯福*在演说中模仿了潘恩的文风，他声明"美国将坚决打败法西斯，让自由普及全世界"[8]。当罗斯福说"让自由普及全世界"时，他提醒了美国人要铭记他们的传统。

潘恩认为北美殖民地的事业就是世界的事业，自由和正义是普世原则，这种价值观已经成为美国民族性格的一部分，罗斯福则使用这种价值观去影响他的听众。因此，我们可以看到，不论是演讲写作，还是政治宣传，《常识》对美国的政治表述有持久的影响。

---

1. 托马斯·潘恩：《常识》，纽约：多弗尔出版公司，1997 年，第 51 页。

2. 埃里克·弗纳：《托马斯·潘恩和革命的美国》，伦敦、纽约和牛津：牛津大学出版社，1976 年，第 85 页。

3. 埃里克·弗纳：《托马斯.潘恩和革命的美国》，第 85 页。

4. 约翰·亚当斯：《致托马斯·杰弗逊》，载《美国第二届总统约翰·亚当斯作品集第十卷：作者生平、笔记和说明》，约翰·亚当斯的孙子查尔斯·弗朗西斯·亚当斯编，波士顿：小布朗出版社，1856 年，http://oll.libertyfund.org/title/2127/193637/3103690，2013 年 9 月 22 日查阅。

5. 索菲亚·罗森菲尔德：《〈常识〉：一部政治史》，马萨诸塞州坎布里奇：哈佛大学出版社，2011 年，第 44 页。

6. 索菲亚·罗森菲尔德：《〈常识〉：一部政治史》，第 54 页。

7. 约翰·孔乐：《托马斯·潘恩的政治人生》，伦敦、纽约和柏林：布鲁姆斯伯里出版社，2009 年，第 295 页。

8. 哈维·J.凯耶引罗斯福，见《托马斯·潘恩与美国的未来》，纽约：希尔与王出版社，2005 年，第 195 页。

8 著作地位

要点 🔑━

- 潘恩相信人拥有某些天赋的权利*，上帝不会干涉人类。

- 《常识》包含潘恩的哲学观念，但是该书的目的却是说服北美进行独立战争。

- 《常识》让潘恩名声大噪，并确立了他在美国历史上的地位。

定位

《常识》是潘恩的第一部重要作品。他早年的政治作品在广度上有限，如 1772 年出版的小册子《海关职员的境况》[1]，他写作或许是出于自我兴趣。他的文章《蚂蚁的军事性格观察》发表在《宾夕法尼亚杂志》1775 年 7 月号上，这是一篇政治讽喻文，其中象征英国军队的红蚂蚁剥夺了黄蚂蚁的天赋权利。由于受英国诽谤法*的限制，潘恩使用了克里奥索[2]这个假名。诽谤法规定，批评政府或者挑起民众藐视国王是违法的。出于同样的原因，《常识》最初匿名出版，然而不久作者的真实身份就被发现。这本小册子对潘恩事业的重要性毋庸赘言，该书"从新闻界脱颖而出，造成的反响如此之大，无论是从著作类型或文字内容来说，在任何时代和任何国家几乎前所未有。"[3]潘恩于是成为名人。

《常识》号召北美民众拿起武器。该书于 1776 年 1 月出版时，莱克星顿和康科德战役*（1775 年 4 月）以及邦克山战役（1775年 6 月）已经发生。该书出版五个月后，《独立宣言》签署，独立革命开弓已无回头箭。1773 至 1776 年间，潘恩一共创作了十六本宣传册，统一被收入《北美危机》中。这些政论文的写作风格都和《常识》相似，都是用来提升北美人民的抗英士气，传播潘恩的哲学思想。

> "潘恩的作品从新闻界脱颖而出，造成的反响如此之大，无论是从著作类型或文字内容来说，在任何时代和任何国家几乎前所未有。"
>
> —— 孟克尔·丹尼尔·康威：《托马斯·潘恩生平》

整合

《常识》在争取北美人民支持独立革命*方面发挥了重要作用。该书的出版建立了潘恩的社会声望，有助于推广他后期的作品。潘恩后期的作品更加全面地解释了他的思想。

潘恩后期的作品声明了他毫不动摇反对君主制和致力于自由事业的立场。作为一名自然神论者*和自由主义者*（指一个人致力于平等和定期选举），潘恩认为人对上帝的信仰应该建立在理性而非传统的基础之上。他将在自己后期具有深远影响的著作《人权论》（1791年）中继续阐述上述思想和其他观点。《人权论》因潘恩的声誉而广为传播，被认为是潘恩对政治哲学最大的贡献。

意义

尽管《常识》让潘恩一举成名，但该书并未全面阐释潘恩的思想观念。潘恩后续的作品才是真正的学术作品，本身也具有很大社会影响，然而读者们应该注意到，正是《常识》的成功才确保了这些作品的出版。潘恩的宣传册具有重要历史影响，因为北美赢得了独立，并建立了一个基于潘恩所论及的自由原则的政府，他的后期著作建立在这种社会声誉之上。

潘恩写作《人权论》是受到了法国大革命 * 的鼓舞。在法国大革命中，法国国王路易十六 * 被处死，人们起草了几部宪法。在《人权论》中，潘恩抨击了世袭继承制和君主制，因为"国王身上具有的暴虐思想和行为会把君主国家搞得四分五裂"[4]。潘恩的另一部重要著作《理性的时代》（1794 年）主要探讨宗教信仰，为自然神论辩护。该书和其他著作不同之处在于它冒着引发宗教争议的风险。通过比较，读者可以发现《常识》包含着宗教温情，这些宗教温情被用来说明独立战争的合理性。人们应该注意到，这些思想是欧洲启蒙运动思想的延续，而非潘恩的独创。

1. 托马斯·潘恩：《托马斯·潘恩作品集》第四卷，孟克尔·丹尼尔·康威主编，纽约：G. P. 普特南父子出版社，1894 年。

2. 爱德华·拉金：《创造美国公众：托马斯·潘恩，宾夕法尼亚杂志和美国独立革命话语》，《美国早期文学》第 33 卷第 3 期，1998 年，第 250—276 页。

3. 孟克尔·丹尼尔·康威：《托马斯·潘恩生平：他在北美、法国及英国的文学、政治和宗教生涯》，后又收入威廉·科伯特的《潘恩素描》，第一卷，纽约：G. P. 普特南父子出版社，1894 年，第 25 页。

4. 托马斯·潘恩：《人权论》，纽约：多弗尔出版公司，1999 年，第 14 页。

第三部分：学术影响

9 最初反响

要点 ⚷

- 同时代的人批评潘恩的《常识》论点肤浅，风格具有煽动性。
- 作家康迪德斯*认为北美殖民地应该继续效忠英国，辩论说反抗者将比国王更加专制。
- 即便那些赞同潘恩北美殖民地应该独立的人也并非都支持北美新政府设置所应采取的形式。

批评

潘恩《常识》的主要批评者是那些北美保皇党人*，即那些希望留在大英帝国的殖民地居民。他们把这本小册子视为危险的作品，认为潘恩"犀利的文笔对于传播非理性和危险的论点非常有用"[1]。保皇党人经常写道，潘恩在书中描绘的社会状况一旦实现会更糟糕，北美反抗者会比英国统治者更加残酷无情。例如，一位使用"康迪德斯"*假名的作家——历史学家们认为此人就是苏格兰出生的军官詹姆斯·查墨斯——警告说如果殖民地居民赢得了抗英战争，他们会更加无情地迫害保皇党人，"（其手段之）狠毒远远超过那些公开拥护专制的人"[2]。

保皇党人批评者来自社会各个阶层[3]，如诗人乔纳森·欧岱尔来自新泽西州，超越社会和地理界限的政治观念将他们联合起来，然而他们的观点对美国独立革命*影响甚微。北美十三个殖民地在潘恩的《常识》出版后不久就宣布独立，就像潘恩所坚持的它们必须独立，于是保皇党人的立场很快就动摇了。

> "(《常识》)是一派拙劣的、无知的、恶意的、目光短浅的酒后胡言。"
>
> —— 约翰·亚当斯:《约翰·亚当斯作品集》

回应

《常识》第二版于 1776 年 2 月出版,潘恩在书中直接回应了批评者。潘恩声称他推迟了第二版的出版,是因为他一直等待着"(保守派)对独立信念的驳斥"[4],但"尚无人作出回应"[5],这表明潘恩藐视批评者的立场。

潘恩没有点名回应批评者,也没有集中讨论某些具体的不同意见。然而我们可以从他的作品中猜想,潘恩知道哪些批评观点需要回答。例如,他对匿名出版的批评回应说,"这部作品的作者是谁,这个问题完全不必要探讨"[6]。对于说他属于某个党派的指控,他认真对待,坚称自己"和任何党派没有瓜葛,也未受任何公众的或个人的影响"[7]。

潘恩也因提出的取代君主制的其他施政形式而受到批评。潘恩辩解说,君主制"已经让世界血流成河生灵涂炭"[8],因此他同样藐视英国的不成文宪法。然而批评家攻击潘恩的施政替代方案是一种共和主义*形式,在这种共和政体中每个公民都对政府事务有发言权。首先,他们指出这种体制在英国革命护国公时期*(1649—1658 年)已经被实践过。当时英国成立了共和国,英国革命将军、政治领导人奥立弗·克伦威尔*担任护国公。保皇党人还指出,克伦威尔自己成了专制者。

其次,根据约翰·亚当斯*的观点,潘恩构想的制度并不比君主制好，因为它保留了"单一国家主体"[9]的权力。亚当斯后来担任美国第二任总统，他赞同"独立的必要性"，也认为"北美有能力维护独立"[10]，但他对新的国家政体应采取的形式有不同看法。他摒弃了潘恩有关直选的立法会的观点，认为所有公民对立法均有话语权行不通[11]。

冲突与共识

潘恩《常识》的写作目的是为了呼唤独立革命，在独立战争真正爆发后，就没有必要出版第三版了。因此我们能够理解，后来者对《常识》的批评都是基于新的政府形式创立后，潘恩书中有些设想没有被采纳。尽管潘恩的设想确实跟政府创立后的形态相像，但他的很多理念被大大地改变了。

亚当斯后来称《常识》"是一派拙劣的、无知的、恶意的、目光短浅的酒后胡言"[12]，他觉得，"不论潘恩是否知道，他顽固坚守大众主权不可分割的思想，有助于拖着共和党人的政治朝着民主的目标又前进了几步"[13]。亚当斯认为自己"把共和主义和民主思想互相冲突的观念区别开来"[14]，他认为潘恩倡导的人人在政府中拥有一票的大众主权思想或政治体制是一个激进的危险的观念。亚当斯认为所有形式的政府，而不仅仅是世袭君主制 *，都容易滥用权力；而且潘恩"忘记了一个基本真理，就是民主把权力集中在多数人的手中，这非常危险"[15]。最为重要的是，亚当斯是新的美国政体构建的核心人物，他的意见举足轻重。

1. 菲利浦·古尔德:《反抗记:保皇党和英属美洲的政治文献》,纽约:牛津大学出版社,2013 年,第 121 页。

2. 詹姆斯·查墨斯:《平凡的真理:写给北美居民的话及对〈常识〉的评论》,南卡罗来纳州查尔斯顿:拉布出版社,2014 年。

3. 辛西亚·都柏林·依黛尔博格:《乔纳森·欧岱尔:美国独立革命中的保皇党诗人》,北卡罗来纳州杜伦:杜克大学出版社,1987 年。

4. 托马斯·潘恩:《常识》,纽约:多弗尔出版公司,1997 年,第 2 页。

5. 托马斯·潘恩:《常识》,第 2 页。

6. 托马斯·潘恩:《常识》,第 2 页。

7. 托马斯·潘恩:《常识》,第 2 页。

8. 托马斯·潘恩:《常识》,第 16 页。

9. 约翰·亚当斯,转引自约翰·孔乐:《托马斯·潘恩的政治人生》,伦敦、纽约和柏林:布鲁姆斯伯里出版社,2009 年,第 125 页。

10. 约翰·孔乐:《托马斯·潘恩的政治人生》,第 125 页。

11. 约翰·孔乐:《托马斯·潘恩的政治人生》,第 125 页。

12. 约翰·亚当斯:《致托马斯·杰弗逊》,载《美国第二届总统约翰·亚当斯作品集第十卷:作者生平,笔记和说明》,约翰·亚当斯的孙子查尔斯·弗朗西斯·亚当斯编,波士顿:小布朗出版社,1856 年,http://oll.libertyfund.org/title/2127/193637/3103690,2013 年 9 月 22 日查阅。

13. 约翰·孔乐:《托马斯·潘恩的政治人生》,第 127 页。

14. 约翰·孔乐:《托马斯·潘恩的政治人生》,第 126 页。

15. 约翰·孔乐:《托马斯·潘恩的政治人生》,第 131 页。

10 后续争议

要点 🔑

- 《常识》给政论文带来了变革，而且形成了北美殖民地和其他地方的政治理念。
- 这本小册子吸收了启蒙运动*的哲学原则。
- 该书集中讨论个体的权利，与美国当今的政治论辩相关。

应用与问题

托马斯·潘恩的政治思想糅合了启蒙运动的各种政治理论，尤其是探讨社会契约论*的理论。尽管这些理论在当时还是纸上谈兵，美国革命战争*却让它们接受检验。潘恩的《常识》最重要、最进步的一面是它采取了超前的思想，并用它去影响社会和政治变革。

简而言之，潘恩的宣传册提出，启蒙运动的重要思想不是抽象的说教，而是影响政府的关键工具。

美国独立战争结束六年后，法国大革命*于1789年爆发，这绝对不是巧合。法国社会的大动荡受到了潘恩在《常识》中学习借鉴的那些哲学家的影响，同时也受到北美发生的真实事件的影响。美国独立后建立了共和国——这是一种国家不需要君主统治的制度。

抛弃了国王和世袭君主制*的共和体制或许是《常识》中最有影响的观念，而且潘恩在《人权论》（1791年）中发展了这个观念。这种制度继续在现代自由民主体制中得到了反映。这就说明共和制的形成并非总能免于困难和阻碍的。例如，曾经担任英国议会议员的埃德蒙·伯克＊经常批评英国的殖民政策。伯克最初支持法国大革命，但是不久他就对法国大革命的血腥感到惊骇。伯克驳斥了天赋人权的观念，反问世人："一个持枪抢劫和谋财害命的杀手，因为他发现了自己的天赋人权而越狱，难道我要向他庆贺？"[1]

> "各个阶层的人带着不同的动机，怀揣不同的设想，都参与了这场争论。但是所有人的争论都是无效的，辩论期结束了。武力是最后可以凭借的资源，它们决定争论的胜负。"
>
> —— 托马斯·潘恩：《常识》

思想流派

潘恩的许多基础性思想都是从他处借鉴而来。我们在阅读《常识》的过程中，经常碰到创立这些思想的启蒙思想家的身影，如政治哲学家托马斯·霍布斯＊、约翰·洛克＊和让-雅克·卢梭＊等。潘恩在书中也探讨了社会契约论，该理论倡导人民放弃部分个人权利，以便形成一个正义的社会，这又让潘恩和后来的思想家产生了关联。一个例证就是法国政治家和自由社会理论家皮艾尔-约瑟夫·蒲鲁东＊。

蒲鲁东创立了一种称之为互助主义的哲学思想，这种思想是基于以下观念：当人们互相依赖的时候，社会才能发挥最好的功能。美国政治哲学家约翰·罗尔斯＊也继承了社会契约论思想流派，他的《正义论》是一部具有争议却受到极大好评的书。该书探讨了社会资源应该如何被最佳分配。

读者应当同时注意到,《常识》对围绕社会契约论的哲学和学术对话影响甚微。然而该书并非为此而作,因为《人权论》才体现了潘恩作为一名政治理论家的地位和影响。《人权论》更全面描述了潘恩的信念,"体现了(潘恩)在大力推广政治国家和国家政治民主化方面的重要性"[2]。

《常识》中最重要的思想就是潘恩如何定义人的自然权利——也就是说,人的自然权利如此重要,以至于它们无法变成法律(因为能立法的话就意味着这些权利可以被剥夺)。美国的建立有助于将这些思想付诸实践,并鼓励其他社会在社会契约论的基础上效仿实施。

当代研究

当代政治学者把潘恩的《常识》当作美国和世界历史上的里程碑。例如,美国威斯康辛大学政治学家哈维·凯*写道:"(潘恩)鼓动北美人民将一场殖民地的反抗变成了独立战争,在民主的广泛性和进步性基础上勾勒了一个新的国家,明确地表明了带有特别目的和前景的美国身份。"[3] 今天,潘恩的思想是如此深刻地影响着我们有关正义和个体权利的信仰,以至于"我们无法理解他的这些思想曾经在历史上引起了一场思维革命"[4]。

潘恩所吸纳的启蒙运动思想对西方政治、文化和政体产生了重要影响。到冷战*——冷战是指苏美两个超级大国在1947至1991年间的紧张对峙——结束时,世界经历了一场美国政治学家弗朗西斯·福山*所描述的"自由主义革命"——这场革命"突破了西欧和北美的滩涂阵地"[5]。

　　福山所指的自由主义 * 虽然不是普世的，但在西方世界得到广泛传播，它反映了潘恩有关自由和政府的理念。只有少数几个西方国家保留了世袭君主制，即便如此（比如英国），这些君主也被剥夺了实权。今天，学者们研究潘恩的《常识》，以了解该书在美国独立战争中的作用以及它对政治演讲和政治写作产生的影响。

---

1. 埃德蒙·伯克：《对法国革命的反思》，牛津：牛津大学出版社，2006 年，第 8 页。

2. 马克·菲利浦：《潘恩著〈权利论〉〈常识〉及其他政治作品导读》，牛津：牛津大学出版社，2008 年，第 XXII 页。

3. 哈维·J. 凯：《托马斯·潘恩和美国的前途》，纽约：希尔与王出版社，2005 年，第 4 页。

4. 克莱格·纳尔逊：《托马斯·潘恩：他的生平、时代和现代国家的诞生》，伦敦：概览书局，2007 年，第 10 页。

5. 弗朗西斯·福山：《历史的终结与最后的人》，伦敦：企鹅书屋，2012 年，第 50 页。

11 当代印迹

要 点 🔑

- 《常识》是美国独立战争 * 史上的里程碑。

- 虽然《常识》的核心思想在当时有些激进，而在当代却似乎很普通。

- 潘恩的论点仍有现实意义，体现在政府对公民行使权力方面。

学术地位

现在潘恩的《常识》最好被看成是一部历史文献。该书给我们讲述了 1775 年在北美受到争论的观念和事件，还向我们展示了启蒙运动 * 的思想原则——比如自然权利 * 是如何启迪了 18 世纪的政治思想。对潘恩来说，专制阻碍了公民的自然权利，这些权利被他写进了一个自由民主的美利坚国家的愿景。

《常识》一书也是美国革命叙事的一部分，历史专业的学生读了此书可以懂得它对美国的形成所作的贡献。潘恩在美国革命的叙事中发挥了重要的作用，这本书读起来很有趣，因为它给我们讲述了有关政治写作和宣传的故事。此外，我们还可以看到潘恩的思想至今如何与自由主义 * 民主还有关联。尽管《常识》和现代自由民主思想有直接关系，但是它不如潘恩的后续作品那么有影响——尤其是《人权论》*（1791 年）。

"《常识》作为一种政治武器的影响力也可以通过很多反对派的效仿者来衡量。他们抓住了这种形式的商业和宣传潜能。"

—— 索菲亚·罗森菲尔德：《〈常识〉：一部政治史》

互动

《常识》对 18 世纪的政治思想的贡献局限于两个方面。首先，潘恩写作此书的目的是为了鼓动民众支持独立，而非影响当时的哲学辩论。此外，《常识》出版后几个月《独立宣言》*就签署了。从那一刻起，美国独立战争已经不可逆转，这使得潘恩的很多观点变得不重要了。

其次，潘恩虽然站在"历史正确的一方"，美国政治学家弗朗西斯·福山*所描述的"世界范围内的自由主义革命"还需要等几个世纪才爆发[1]，直到 20 世纪世袭君主制*政府才被时代抛弃。类似地，潘恩的著作没有对帝国主义*产生直接的影响——在帝国主义政治中，某些国家通过外交和军事力量向其他国家施加权力和影响——尽管潘恩批评英国殖民统治的立论基础之一就是帝国主义。

这就是说，潘恩的世界观最终经受了时间的检验。今天自由主义的民主政治一般容许个体的自然权利和政府的权力和平共处——这种观念与《常识》的精髓吻合。在 21 世纪，很少有人赞同一个国家统治另外一个国家，拒绝给它代表权，并且征收不公正的税收之类的观念。此外，也没有很多人支持回到前民主政府的时代。今天赞成这样开历史倒车的知识分子都被排除在严肃的学术探讨的边缘，或者被看成是政治极端主义分子。因此潘恩的政治遗产在当今各种常见的政府体制中得到体现。

持续争议

如今有关个体权利的论辩还在持续。西方世界开始抨击那种不保障公民的自然权利的国家观。当代法国文化学家保罗·维利里奥*的精神污染学说*可以解释这种行为，该学说认为新技术让各种思想传播得更快更远。这就是为什么西方思潮，比如受启蒙运动所影响的思潮，具有广泛吸引力的一个原因。[2]

---

1. 弗朗西斯·福山：《历史的终结与最后的人》，伦敦：企鹅书屋，2012 年，第 39 页。
2. 保罗·维利里奥：《信息炸弹》，克里斯·特纳翻译，伦敦：维尔索出版公司，2015 年，第 15 页。

12 未来展望

要点 🔑

- 潘恩的《常识》对理解美国独立革命非常重要，而且现在人们还在研究它的戏剧化的煽动性的檄文风格。
- 《常识》将继续被看成是鼓励北美殖民地独立的主要精神源泉之一。
- 对于那些想了解为什么北美殖民地会和英国开战的人来说，《常识》是指定读物。

潜力

潘恩的《常识》未来很可能依旧是一本具有重要影响的读物。尽管它不是一部伟大的哲学著作，但是在激励民众支持北美殖民地脱离大英帝国独立方面发挥了重要作用，因而具有重要的历史地位。因为《常识》被广泛阅读，潘恩因普及启蒙运动*的重要思想值得世人尊重。

《常识》非常重要，因为该书的思想观念被写入支撑美国创立的两份基础性政治文件——美国宪法*和《独立宣言》*。后来成为美国第三任总统的托马斯·杰弗逊*在上述两份历史文献中强调了"自然权利"*的重要性。

> "（潘恩）鼓动北美人民将一场殖民地的反抗变成了独立战争，在民主的广泛性和进步性基础上勾勒了一个新的国家，明确地表明了带有特别目的和前景的美国身份。"
> —— 哈维·J. 凯：《托马斯·潘恩和美国的前途》

未来方向

潘恩的核心思想不会再发生改变，也不再引起争论，而且他倡导的大部分观念都已广泛实现：包含容许公民享有自然权利的政体，终结世袭君主制*，自由选举，当然还有美国的独立。在今天的自由主义*民主国家中，这些思想归于美国传播学专家丹尼尔·C.哈林*描述的"共识圈"[1]，因为它们鲜为人们质疑。

综上所述，《常识》标志着历史的转折点。潘恩朴实而平易的写作风格于今已经变成政治演说的共同特点。就《常识》的思想内容而言，读者要尽力去理解为什么这本书当年引起了那么多的争论，这就表明潘恩思想的影响力之大。今天，自由主义的民主国家实现了《常识》大部分的诉求，如果不是全部的话。《常识》因为对专制政体的批评而引发读者共鸣。潘恩对正义的辩护启迪人心，而且提醒我们，美国的独立事业过去是——现在仍然是一项崇高的事业。

结语

潘恩的《常识》和18世纪的其他政治作品不同，因为它具有易读性和煽动性的散文风格。潘恩抨击了任何与他相左的观点。他不仅吸收了英国启蒙运动哲学家约翰·洛克*的激进*观点，而且将这些思想发挥到极致——那就是，如果君主破坏了社会契约*，他们可以被取代掉。潘恩鄙视英国国王乔治三世*，嘲笑世袭君主制，最终他让读者明白不服从英国的统治是可以被接受的。

《常识》获得成功，不是因为它的学识成就，而是因为潘恩抓住了对北美殖民地普通居民来说最重要的东西。在这个意义上，

《常识》是一部杰作，它帮助把启蒙运动的思想原则传播给普通读者。如果有人想要了解北美殖民地的独立战争，新的美国政府的形成，以及美国政体如何影响世界上其他国家，这本书对于他们来说非常重要。潘恩辩论说，"美国的独立事业在很大程度上说就是人类的事业"。[2] 他的观点都被历史验证为正确，如同他的很多其它预言一样。

美国的建立极大地影响了当今自由主义的民主国家。

---

1. 丹尼尔·C.哈林：《未被审查的战争：媒体和越南》，伯克利：加利福尼亚大学出版社，1989 年，第 116 页。
2. 托马斯·潘恩：《常识》，纽约：多弗尔出版公司，1997 年，第 2 页。

术语表

1. **美国革命战争**（1775—1783）：英国和北美英属十三个殖民地之间的军事冲突。最终法国、西班牙与荷兰也卷入了战争。也被称为美国独立战争。

2. **无政府状态**：个人不承认权威和政府而造成的混乱状态。有些政治学家把基于公民自治的个人自由放在首位，拒绝政府存在的需要。他们认同无政府状态是一种社会组织形式。

3. **波士顿茶叶党事件**：也称为波士顿倾茶事件。1773 年 12 月 16 日，北美殖民地的示威者们登上停泊在波士顿港的三艘英国商船，将船上托运来的茶叶倾入波士顿湾，以此抗议英国 1773 年颁布的《茶税法》。《茶税法》规定英国政府有权在北美殖民地征税，扩大财政收入。

4. **大英帝国**：英国在 16 世纪至 18 世纪期间建立的一个海洋帝国或海军帝国，包括加拿大、澳大利亚、新西兰、南非、印度以及后来独立的北美十三州等地区和殖民地。

5. **火烧法尔茅斯**：发生在 1775 年 10 月的事件。当时英国海军轰炸了法尔茅斯，该地原属马萨诸塞州，现在属缅因州。

6. **《强制法案》**：支持革命的北美殖民地民众俗称其为"不可容忍法案"，是强加给北美殖民地马萨诸塞州的一系列法律。该法案规定马萨诸塞州将直接接受英国国王乔治三世委任的官员统治。

7. **冷战**（1947—1991）：1947 年至 1991 年期间美苏之间的紧张局势。冷战没有导致美苏两国之间的战争，但是实施了间谍活动和

代理人战争。

8. **君主立宪制**：这是一种政府组织形式，通过立宪限制君主权力。

9. **《独立宣言》**：北美十三个殖民地宣告从大英帝国脱离的文告。1776年7月4日，《独立宣言》由第二届大陆会议批准。

10. **自然神论**：对上帝的信仰应建立在理性而非传统基础之上的观念。

11. **英国自由**：对国王权力的限制，比如案件交给陪审团审判的权力，限制君主加税的权力。

12. **启蒙运动**：17世纪至18世纪发生在欧洲的一场思想运动。该运动挑战当时人们普遍信奉的建立在传统和宗教基础之上的思想观念，并试图通过科学和理性推进知识发展。

13. **第一届大陆会议**：北美殖民地于1774年9月至10月召开的一次联合会议。十三个殖民地的12名代表（乔治亚州未派代表参加）与会，向英国国王乔治三世发出请愿，纠正对殖民地的各种不公。

14. **法国大革命（1789—1799）**：1789至1799年间法国爆发的社会动荡与政治运动，最后导致法国国王路易十六被处死，其间起草并颁布了几部临时宪法。

15. **文法学校**：一种学校类型。潘恩所处时代的文法学校是指那些教授圣经、拉丁文、希腊文和数学等有限课程的私立学校。

16. **世袭君主制**：一种王权按照血统关系世代传承，王位通常由最大的男性继承人继承的政体形式。

17. **精神污染或意识形态污染**：新技术使得思想观念能够快速地从一个地方传播到另外一个地方的过程。

18. **帝国主义**：一个国家通过经济、外交和军事手段及政策对其他国家施加权力和影响的形态。

19. **莱克星顿战役和康科德战役**：1775 年 4 月发生在波士顿附近的两次战役，当英军试图摧毁北美民兵的军事仓库的时候，他们受到了当地民众的抵抗，爆发了战斗。

20. **诽谤**：某些法律裁定批评当时政府、挑起人民憎恨或者蔑视君主的行为是非法的。匿名出版成为一种常见的策略用以免遭逮捕。

21. **自由主义**：一种强调自由、平等、定期竞争性选举的政治哲学。

22. **保皇党**：一部分希望留在大英帝国内的北美殖民地居民。

23. **自然权利**：普遍固有的绝对权利，人人生而具有，比如追求幸福的权利等。这些权利区别于法律权利。

24. **和平主义或反战主义**：反对战争或暴力的哲学理念。

25. **博学之士**：拥有跨专业知识的人。

26. **总统制**：一种由总统为首的政府形式，总统由人民或人民代表选举产生。

27. **护国公时期**：1649 至 1658 年期间的英国。当时英国为共和国，奥利弗·克伦威尔任护国公执政。

28. **贵格会**：兴起于 17 世纪英国的基督教分支，反对战争和暴力。

29. **激进主义**：任何形式的激进自由主义意识形态。《常识》出版时，激进主义是指当时北美殖民地居民想脱离英国，以建立一个更加公正的社会。

30. **现实政治**：19 世纪的一个术语，指从实用角度去考虑政治行动是否可以实现，与从道德或意识形态出发采取行动相对。

31. **共和主义**：一种拒绝接受世袭君主制的意识形态。

32. **《人权论》**：1791 年潘恩出版此书，以回应 1789 年发生的法国大革命，以及哲学家埃德蒙·伯克撰写的《对法国革命的反思》一书对法国大革命的批评。潘恩在书中声言，如果一个政府不能够或者不愿意保障公民的基本权利或自然权利，革命可以被接受。

33. **第二届大陆会议**：1775 年 5 月召开的北美殖民地代表会议，以组织抵抗英国从此大陆会议成为北美殖民地临时政府机构。

34. **七年战争（1754—1763）**：1754 至 1763 年间英国和法国为了贸易利益在各自帝国领土上发生的军事冲突。

35. **社会契约论**：一种哲学思想，认为人的天性由理性支配，人们为了接受管理而必须放弃的权利数量是有限的。

36. **苏联（1922—1991）**：指位于欧亚大陆的苏维埃社会主义共和国联盟。1917 年俄国革命后在俄罗斯帝国基础上创立。苏联是当时世界上最大的国家。后成为超级大国，冷战时期与美国对峙。

37. **自然状态**：一种哲学家使用的思想实验，以描述人类群体社会形成

前的生活样态。

38. **1773 年茶税法案**：英国政府颁布的一系列法案之一，为扩大财政收入服务，规定英国有权在北美殖民地收税。波士顿倾茶事件系对此法案的反应。

39. **美国宪法**：美国的最高法律文件，1790 年在第二届大陆会议上被全部十三个州批准。美国宪法规定了未来美国政府的形式，承诺保障每个公民的某些权利。

人名表

1. 约翰·亚当斯（1735—1826），美国独立革命的重要领导人，美国第二任总统。启蒙思想原则的支持者，曾严厉批评潘恩的许多思想。

2. 埃德蒙·伯克（1729—1797），爱尔兰政治理论家，以《对法国革命的反思》一书著称。

3. 康迪德斯，1776 年出版的《平凡的真理》小册子作者使用的假名。尽管无人有确切把握，人们猜测作者可能是马里兰保皇党人詹姆斯·查墨斯。

4. 奥利弗·克伦威尔（1599—1658），英国十七世纪政治和军事领袖，他在英国内战（1642—1651）后，出任护国公。去世后共和国垮台。新的国王查理二世继承了王位。

5. 埃里克·弗纳（1943 年生），美国历史学家，托马斯·潘恩的传记作者。以有关政治历史的著作而闻名。

6. 本杰明·富兰克林（1706—1790），美国开国元勋、政治鼓动家、科学家、作家。他在独立战争时期致力于维护北美殖民地团结，后担任首任美国驻法国大使。

7. 弗朗西斯·福山（1952 年生），美国政治学家，代表作是《历史的终结与最后一人》。他倡导自由民主和自由市场经济，认为这是组织社会的终极手段。

8. 乔治三世（1738—1820），大不列颠国王，1776 年《独立宣言》签署前北美十三个殖民地的统治者。他拒绝听取北美殖民地居民的呼声和要求，最终导致美国独立战争爆发。

9. **胡果·格劳秀斯**（1583—1645），荷兰哲学家，提出天赋人权和不可被剥夺的自然权利等观点，为社会契约论奠定了基础。

10. **丹尼尔·C.哈林**，圣迭戈大学媒介与传播研究员，以研究媒体如何反映社会规约的作品而受推崇。

11. **约瑟夫·休斯**（1730—1779），北美殖民地卡罗莱纳贵格会会员，《独立宣言》签署者之一，他还积极参加了北美大陆会议。

12. **克里斯托弗·希金斯**（1949—2011），一名高产作家和新闻记者，自称是社会主义者。希金斯对许多历史人物采取了与世不同的批评态度，比如对特蕾莎修女和教皇本笃十六世等。

13. **托马斯·霍布斯**（1588—1679），英国哲学家，以其作品《利维坦》著称。通过该书他确立了社会契约论，他捍卫政府（尤其是君主制），把政府当作抵抗混乱的"自然状态"的最高武器。

14. **托马斯·杰弗逊**（1743—1826），美国开国元勋，《独立宣言》的主要起草者，后任美国第三任总统。

15. **哈维·J.凯**，威斯康辛大学民主和正义学乔伊斯·罗森伯格荣誉教授，出版过两本有关潘恩的著作。

16. **约翰·孔乐**，澳大利亚政治学研究者，悉尼大学和德国柏林研究中心政治学教授，目前主要研究亚太地区。

17. **约翰·洛克**（1632—1704），英国哲学家，现代自由主义思想之父。他认为人的天性是由理性支配，人的部分而非全部自由要让渡给国家。代表作《政府论》（1689年）被认为是政治思想的里程碑。

18. **法国国王路易十六**（1754—1793），1774—1792年间法国国王，1792年在法国大革命中被废黜，1793年接受审判后被处死。

19. 乔纳森·欧岱尔（1737—1818），北美殖民地诗人，因忠于英国，在美国独立革命后受到了法律处罚。

20. 皮埃尔-约瑟夫·蒲鲁东（1809—1865），法国政治家、自由社会理论家，互助主义哲学观念的创建者，他是第一个称自己无政府主义者的人。

21. 约翰·罗尔斯（1921—2002），美国哲学家，民主政治的支持者。他最著名的作品《正义论》出版于1971年，受到学术批评界一致好评。

22. 富兰克林·罗斯福（1882—1945），美国第三十二任总统，优秀的演说家，是美国唯一连任四届的总统（1933—1945）。

23. 索菲亚·罗森菲尔德，美国弗吉尼亚大学历史系教授，主要研究政治话语、语言学和革命分析。

24. 让-雅克·卢梭（1712—1778），日内瓦派哲学家、启蒙运动思想家，他的著作极大地影响了法国大革命，其中《论人类不平等的起源》与《社会契约论》两书均为现代政治思想的基石。

25. 保罗·维利里奥（1932年生），法国文化理论家，对技术的后果进行哲学思考。意识形态污染是他提出的最重要观点之一，认为技术导致不同文化之间思想的自由交流。

26. 伏尔泰（1694—1778），原名弗朗索瓦-玛利·阿鲁埃，伏尔泰是他的笔名。法国启蒙运动作家，倡导个体权利，主张政教分离，他1756年发表的《论民族的精神和习俗》影响了思想家观察历史的方式。

27. 乔治·华盛顿（1732—1799），参加过法国-印第安战争，莱克星顿和康科德战役后不久，他于1775年6月14日出任美国大陆军总司令。1789年当选为美国第一任总统。

WAYS IN TO THE TEXT

- Though born in England in 1737, Thomas Paine is best remembered for writing pamphlets that inspired Americans to revolt against Great Britain.

- *Common Sense* called for American independence and explained how to achieve it.

- Paine's pamphlet made political ideas accessible and sold in huge numbers. It directly influenced the outcome of the American Revolution*—the military conflict that led to the independence of 13 of Great Britain's North American colonies and the formation of the United States of America.

Who Was Thomas Paine?

Thomas Paine was born in England in 1737. His father belonged to the Quakers,* a denomination of Christianity that opposes war and violence. Though few received an education at this time, and Paine's family was not rich, he attended a grammar school*—what we would today call a "secondary" or "high" school—until he was 13. There he received a basic education in Latin, Greek, mathematics, and the Scriptures.

Paine's early life was not particularly successful. Neither of his marriages lasted, and the businesses he started failed. In 1772, while working for the Customs and Excise Office inspecting imported goods, Paine wrote his first political work, *The Case of the Officers of Excise*, in which he argued for better working conditions and pay. He was dismissed from this post early in 1774.

In September 1774, Paine was introduced to Benjamin

Franklin,* an inventor, author, and political agitator who would become one of the Founding Fathers of the United States of America. Franklin was impressed with Paine, and he not only advised him to move to North America, but also gave him a letter of recommendation.

When Paine arrived in Philadelphia, the political situation in the American colonies was quite volatile. The Seven Years War,* fought between Great Britain and France over conflicting trade interests, had ended 11 years earlier. While Great Britain had won, it was heavily in debt and wanted the colonies to help cover the war's cost. Paine, like many Americans, was outraged that Britain would tax the colonies to help pay for the war while refusing them representation in Parliament. He felt that America must become independent, and he made his case in *Common Sense*.

What Does *Common Sense* Say?

Paine believed that the American colonies could win independence despite a military disadvantage. At the time, the most important part of a country's military was its navy, and Britain had the best navy in the world. However, Paine claimed that America had many advantages over Britain. For example, it was rich in natural resources like trees, which were needed to build ships. Additionally, British soldiers would have to travel a great distance to reach the fighting.

More important was Paine's argument that British rule was unfair. He wanted to create a free society in which decisions were made not by a king or queen, but by the people. The ideas in

Common Sense were easy to understand, and they still influence American politics today. Because of this, *Common Sense* is an important part of American history.

The ideas were not Paine's alone. He drew from a European intellectual movement called the Enlightenment* that emphasized reason and individualism over tradition. Among the interests of Enlightenment thinkers was a general inquiry into how societies could be fairer. Nobody, however, had yet tried to organize a society based on Enlightenment principles.

Paine helped change that. After winning the Revolution, American society was formed around the sorts of personal freedom for which Enlightenment thinkers argued. While some believed such a system would lead to chaos, America's success proved them wrong. Paine is considered one of the Founding Fathers of the United States because of his pamphlet's role in these political changes.

Those studying Paine should see *Common Sense* as valuable for two reasons. First, it helps us understand the fears and thoughts that average eighteenth-century colonists had about their political situation. It also shows us why even some who were not happy with recent events wanted to stay part of the British Empire.* Second, Paine's writing style influenced the way future political arguments were made. He took the political opinion of elite thinkers and made them accessible to anyone who could read. As the political historian Eric Foner* notes, Paine "communicated a new vision" of government not just to a broad American audience, but to a worldwide audience.[1]

Why Does *Common Sense* Matter?

Common Sense listed reasons in favor of American independence and attacked those who wanted to remain British subjects. As such, the text provides the reader with a sense of the eighteenth-century public's feeling and mood. It can therefore help students understand both history and politics. It can also help explain why freedom is considered to be so important to so many today.

Common Sense was innovative because it made difficult ideas easy to understand. These ideas would outlast the Revolution and become part of everyday politics. For example, Paine's ideas made their way into both the Declaration of Independence* (the statement issued by 13 British colonies to the British Empire in which they declared that they considered themselves independent) and the US Constitution* (the document setting out the rights of American citizens and the nature and obligations of their government). Both documents formed the basis for the American system of government; the Constitution has proven to be enormously influential globally.

Paine also popularized ideas that had previously been understood only by a few well-educated people. For example, he explained that freedom of religion and freedom of speech were not dangerous, as was thought at the time, but would lead to a better world.

Paine's style also showed that it was beneficial for political writing to be easy to read. The pamphlet sold in large numbers, and the war would not have had so much support without it.

Additionally, this support allowed American leaders to put these new ideas into place after the war was over. The success of the new American system caused some Europeans to think about making similar changes. The old argument that a free country would be a horrible place looked weak, and people began to want more from their governments. In this way, we can see how Paine's *Common Sense* drastically affected how people throughout the world saw political systems.

---

1. Eric Foner, *Tom Paine and Revolutionary America* (London, New York, and Oxford: Oxford University Press, 1976), xvi.

SECTION 1
INFLUENCES

THE AUTHOR AND THE HISTORICAL CONTEXT

KEY POINTS

- *Common Sense* was instrumental in inspiring popular support for independence.

- Paine immigrated in 1774 to America, where he could argue for his ideas to be put into practice.

- The American Revolutionary War* (the military conflict between 13 colonies of the British Empire and the empire's army that led to the formation of the young United States) provided the chance to create a nation based on the principles of the Enlightenment*—a movement in European culture and thinking towards rationality and individualism.

Why Read This Text?

Thomas Paine first published *Common Sense* in 1776. His pamphlet argues that the political and economic union of America and Britain "sooner or later must have an end."[1] Paine critiques Britain's hereditary monarchy*—a system in which sovereign power is inherited by succeeding generations of the same family—and asserts that it is impractical for a small, distant island to govern a continent. He claimed that Britain had inflicted economic and social injustices upon the colonists that were an affront to their personal freedoms.

While many in America accepted that grievances existed between Britain and the colonies, some believed that reconciliation was possible. However, Paine argued that "everything that is right or natural pleads for separation,"[2] and insisted that independence was the best course of action. His arguments led to a notable shift in the attitudes of colonists, who began to support revolution in much larger numbers. It should be noted that the primary purpose of *Common Sense* was propaganda. That is, it was not written to provide unbiased information, but rather to convince its audience that Paine was right.

Paine's text offers a brief summary of eighteenth-century political ideas and helps make contemporary political thought easy to understand. Additionally, *Common Sense* helps us understand how the American Revolution succeeded. This is important because the revolution influenced Western political systems in ways that still reverberate today.

"Everything that is right or natural pleads for separation."

Thomas Paine, *Common Sense*

Author's Life

Paine was born in England in 1737 to a Quaker* father and an Anglican mother. His early life was undistinguished. Until he was 13 he attended grammar school,* where he received a basic education. His first marriage ended tragically, when his wife and daughter died during childbirth. Paine's second marriage to Elizabeth Olive lasted only four years, and they formally separated in 1774. His business ventures, such as his tobacco shop, also failed.

Paine's first notable experiment with writing came while working at the Custom and Excise Office in London. He wrote a 21-page pamphlet, *The Case of the Officers of Excise*, in which he argued for better working conditions and an increased salary. He was dismissed from this post shortly after its publication.

Paine's life changed when he was introduced to the American political theorist and scientist Benjamin Franklin* in September 1774. Little is known about this meeting, but Paine set sail for Philadelphia almost immediately after it. He arrived on November 30 and soon became a citizen. Franklin had given Paine a letter of recommendation—an important endorsement at the time. By January 1775, Paine was employed as the editor of a periodical called the *Pennsylvania Magazine*. Here, he immersed himself in American politics and developed his unique style.

Author's Background

America was still a sovereign territory of Great Britain when Paine arrived in 1774. It was also in the midst of a crisis. Britain and France had fought for control of America in what was known in Europe as the Seven Years War,* and though Britain had won, the war had been expensive. As a consequence, Britain imposed taxes on the colonies to help pay its debts. The colonists were outraged that the government could tax them without their consent, especially given that they had been denied representation in the British Parliament.

The political situation deteriorated further after the Boston Tea Party* of 1773, in which colonists boarded three British ships in Boston Harbor and threw the consignment of tea overboard. The British response was to pass a series of five laws, called the Coercive Acts,[*3] which were designed to punish the colonies and reestablish control over the territories. Massachusetts, one of the more rebellious states, was targeted in particular. For instance, the acts closed Boston's port, gave direct control of the Massachusetts government to a British-appointed governor, gave the governor the right to insist that accused government officials be tried in Great Britain, and permitted the governor to house troops in unoccupied buildings.

Unsurprisingly, the new laws provoked outrage: the colonists referred to them as the "Intolerable Acts." As a result, the First Continental Congress* was organized, in which representatives from 12 of the 13 colonies (Georgia did not attend) met in Philadelphia from September to October 1774. Coincidentally, this was almost exactly when Paine arrived in the city.

The congress sent a petition to Britain's king, George III,* asking him to address their grievances with the Coercive Acts and various other issues. After the petition was rejected, the Second Continental Congress* met in May 1775 to prepare for the war effort that many, though not all, now saw as inevitable.

The battles of Lexington and Concord* had been fought on April 19, 1775, and these first conflicts effectively began the American Revolutionary War. On July 4, 1776, the Second Continental Congress issued the Declaration of Independence,* which declared that the 13 colonies were no longer part of the British Empire.

---

1. Thomas Paine, *Common Sense* (New York: Dover Publications Inc., 1997), 22.

2. Paine, *Common Sense,* 22.

3. Only four of the five acts were in direct response to the general sense of rebellion. The fifth was related to the borders of Quebec.

ACADEMIC CONTEXT

KEY POINTS

- *Common Sense* discussed what should be done about the political crises unfolding in the American colonies.

- Thinkers of the Enlightenment*—the current of European thought that increasingly stressed rationality and individualism—emphasized the rights of the individual over the power of the state.

- Paine was self-taught and had no formal education in political philosophy.

The Work in its Context

In *Common Sense*, Thomas Paine appealed to a sense of national pride that existed in Britain's colonies in the eighteenth century. Although his writing reflected "the consensus opinion of his Enlightenment peers,"[1] Paine's goal was not to educate but to inspire political change. He wrote so that the common colonist could grasp his meaning, mixing straightforward arguments with biblical references, and appealing to how colonists felt about the political climate.

Paine chose not to mention Enlightenment philosophers such as the British political philosopher John Locke,* the Genevan political philosopher Jean-Jacques Rousseau,* and the French political philosopher and writer Voltaire,* and others more immediate to Paine's circle, such as the American political theorist and scientist Benjamin Franklin.* However, it is easy to see how he was influenced by these thinkers, given what they contributed to eighteenth-century thought.

Locke is often considered the father of modern liberalism,* and, along with Voltaire, argued for the rights of the individual and the separation of church and state. Rousseau's writing on social inequality and political systems would influence both the American Revolution* (in which the young United States forcibly took its independence from the British Empire*) and the French Revolution* (in which French citizens rose up to overturn the social order, overthrowing the monarchy and instituting a republic).

Ideas about individual rights and freedoms were not immediately accessible to the average person in the eighteenth century. The American colonies were subject to the king of England, and though his power was not absolute, colonists were still limited in what they could do and say. Unlike today, no real alternative to this system of government had been attempted. As such, it was difficult for those in favor of individual liberty to answer those who argued that individual liberties would lead to anarchy.*

> "But where, says some, is the King of America? I'll tell you friend, he reigns above and doth not make havoc of mankind like the Royal Brute of Britain."
>
> Thomas Paine, *Common Sense*

Overview of the Field

The intellectual climate of the time was volatile, as Enlightenment thinkers were challenging existing beliefs about religion, government, and individual rights. Like Voltaire, Paine was a deist,* meaning that he believed that reason rather than tradition should be the foundation for belief in God. He also believed that reason and not tradition should be the basis of government.Though he did state these claims explicitly in *Common Sense*, it is still possible to see the influences of Enlightenment thinkers in the subtext of the pamphlet.

An idea central to *Common Sense*, and to all Enlightenment political thought, is the social contract*—the idea, established by the English philosopher Thomas Hobbes,* that human nature is governed by reason, and that there is a limit to the number of rights citizens should consent to lose for the sake of good governance; Hobbes believed that human beings would live in chaos unless subject to strong authoritative governments like monarchies.

Paine agreed with Hobbes that some form of government was necessary for civil society, but he strongly disagreed about how much was required. Paine argued not only that were men free, equal, and independent, but also that their only king was God, who reigned above and "doth not make havoc of mankind like the Royal Brute of Britain."[2]

John Locke was another important influence on Paine. Locke believed that human nature was governed by reason, and he argued for a form of government in which people voluntarily abandoned personal liberties in order to create a civil society. Locke had argued that people should give up fewer rights than Hobbes thought they should, and Paine took this even further. According to Paine, citizens should give up as few rights as possible—and some rights could not be given up at all, not even by choice.

Although Paine recognized that societies needed leaders, he wanted a presidential system,* in which the leader is elected by the people, and not a hereditary monarchy,* in which authority stays within a family and is passed from generation to generation. Furthermore, he believed that the presidency should be both temporary and limited in power.[3] In *Common Sense*, Paine argued that his ideas should be put into place. The pamphlet was not just a contribution to philosophical debate.

Academic Influences

While we have seen that Enlightenment thinking influenced Paine, it is possible to look more closely at his principles. He believed in liberalism, a political philosophy that emphasizes freedom, equality, and regularly contested elections. He was also influenced by republicanism,* an ideology that rejects the notion that the head of state should be a hereditary position, such as that of a king or other monarch. Finally, he was a radical,* which at the time referred to those who wished to break with England in order to create a fairer society. Today, it should be noted, radicalism has come to mean any form of extreme ideology. Paine may also have learned a great deal from Benjamin Franklin, who was a politician of considerable influence, as well as a polymath* (that is, his expertise spanned several fields of knowledge).

Paine's Enlightenment peers had been struggling with how best to organize society for some time. Hobbes had felt that without an authoritative ruler, the strong would dominate or enslave the weak. As a result, he thought that life was the only inalienable, or guaranteed, right that people had. Locke was less extreme. He wrote that people had a range of incontestable rights, but that they still had to trade some for security and peace.

According to Paine, however, Hobbes's monarch was a tyrant, and Locke's constitutional monarchy,* in which the power of the monarch was limited by a constitution, was not much better. Paine melded these ideas with more modern thinking, such as that of Jean-Jacques Rousseau, who argued for democratic rule. Though this does not seem radical today, it contradicted the common wisdom of the day.

---

1. Craig Nelson, *Thomas Paine: His Life, His Time and the Birth of Modern Nations* (London: Profile Books, 2007), 8.
2. Thomas Paine, *Common Sense* (New York: Dover Publications Inc., 1997), 31.
3. Paine, *Common Sense*, 30.

MODULE 3
THE PROBLEM

KEY POINTS

* Paine wanted to guarantee the rights of the individual above all else.

* In most European countries, the individual was less important than loyalty to one's king or nation.

* Paine made it possible for anyone to understand the debate over individual rights.

Core Questions

Thomas Paine's *Common Sense* tried to answer two core questions. First, was independence from Britain desirable? Second, was it achievable?

Paine intended his pamphlet to serve as propaganda; he believed "yes" was the answer to both questions and made no attempt to offer a balanced discussion. He began writing shortly after the American Revolution* began, although at the time, many, including some in the Continental Congress,* still hoped for reconciliation. This is why these core questions were so important: Paine's primary purpose was to convince both the masses and American leaders that independence was the correct course of action.

Paine said British rule amounted to tyranny. He was less clear on whether independence could be achieved. At the time, defeat was a serious possibility. Given what we know now, it is easy to miss how much Paine's argument was a monumental gamble. That the gamble paid off remains one of the more compelling reasons why *Common Sense* has endured.

> "As in absolute governments the king is law so too in free countries the law ought to be king."
>
> Thomas Paine, *Common Sense*

The Participants

Although *Common Sense* does not refer to specific political or philosophical theories, Paine's intellectual influences are clear. One important thinker whose ideas we find reflected in the pamphlet is the English philosopher John Locke.*

Locke's concept of a civilized society was based on natural rights,* or rights that should be guaranteed to all people, and social contract theory,* which was the idea that some liberties should be given up for the sake of a peaceful, just society.

Paine took Locke's belief that only consent could "give a man permanent membership of society," and expressed it in language that was deliberately inflammatory.[1] For example, Paine wrote that independence meant "no more than, whether we shall make our own laws or, whether the King, the greatest enemy this continent hath or can have shall tell us 'there shall be no laws but such as I like'."[2] Most Enlightenment* texts were not nearly so provocative, because they were directed at an intellectual audience and their authors, who feared arrest, tended to be more cautious.

Not every Enlightenment thinker believed in the same version of social contract theory, and Paine drew from a range of sources. Another of his influences was the philosopher Jean-Jacques Rousseau,* who was born in Geneva, in what is now Switzerland. In *Du Contrat social*, Rousseau claimed that it was important for citizens to obey the law for the collective good of society.[3] Like Rousseau, Paine believed in the importance of laws based on reason, writing that "as in absolute governments the king is law so too in free countries the law ought to be king."[4]

He differed from Rousseau in that he valued individual rights over the collective good. Paine dismissed the question of what rights colonists should give up entirely, since he did not think English law was legitimate: "[you] that oppose independence now [you] know not what [you] do," he wrote; "[you] are opening a door to eternal tyranny by leaving vacant the seat of government."[5]

In making this statement, he further radicalized* what were already extreme ideas. *Common Sense* thus attacks British rule both by asking what rights citizens should give up to their rulers, and who should be permitted to rule in the first place.

The Contemporary Debate

When Paine published *Common Sense* in 1776, the intellectual battlefield included a volatile mix of Enlightenment ideas, traditional thinking, and realpolitik* ideas (that is, ideas governed by practical concerns rather than moral considerations). Paine drew on this debate, often taking radical ideas and making them even more extreme.

For example, John Locke believed that monarchs should have their power limited by a constitution. Paine took this further, ridiculing even the concept of a constitutional monarchy:* "Why is the constitution of England sickly, but because monarchy hath poisoned the republic, the crown hath engrossed the commons?"[6] Similarly, the French philosopher Voltaire* believed that England was freer than France because of its constitutional monarchy. Paine, however, openly dismissed the idea that English liberties had any real substance.

Even supporters of independence such as the politician John Adams,* who was to be the second president of the United States, thought *Common Sense* was too radical. According to Adams, Paine tended to resort to false dichotomies, or claiming that only two choices exist when in reality there are many possibilities. In *Thoughts on Government* (1776), Adams rejected Paine's idea that the country could be governed by a single legislative body. He wrote that people could not "be long free, nor ever happy, whose government is in one assembly."[7]

To understand *Common Sense* today, the reader must have some understanding of Enlightenment thought. It is important to remember that while Paine borrowed ideas, he took the time to trace their origins, as he wanted his pamphlet to be simple and accessible.

Finally, one reason why Paine's ideas were often more extreme than those whose work he drew on was the context in which he wrote. Those writing in Europe could afford to make abstract arguments. Paine's ideas had to be immediately applied to the volatile political situation in the colonies; there was so very little time for debate.

1. John Locke, *Two Treatises of Government*, ed. Peter Laslett (Cambridge: Cambridge University Press, 1988), 111.

2. Thomas Paine, Common Sense (New York: Dover Publications Inc., 1997), 27.

3. Christopher D. Wraight, *Rousseau's* The Social Contract: *A Reader's Guide* (New York: Continuum, 2008), 33.

4. Paine, Common Sense, 31–2.

5. Paine, Common Sense, 33.

6. Paine, Common Sense, 17.

7. John Adams, *Thoughts on Government*, accessed November 7, 2013, http://www.constitution.org/jadams/thoughts.htm.

THE AUTHOR'S CONTRIBUTION

KEY POINTS

* Paine believed that the only interest government should serve was the will of the people.

* By putting Enlightenment* ideas into practice, Paine contributed significantly to the formation of the United States.

* Paine understood the need to translate abstract philosophical ideas into practical ones in order to cause political change.

Author's Aims

In writing *Common Sense*, Thomas Paine was aware of the limits of his intended audience. The philosophical ideas that informed his work were not familiar to the average person in 1776—and nor were they easily explained. Thus his text was not a philosophical treatise but a call for political action. It was written clearly and concisely, avoiding complex metaphors and intricate arguments.

Because literacy was uncommon in eighteenth-century New England, there were also restrictions on the pamphlet's length. *Common Sense* was intended to be read aloud at public gatherings, which would have been difficult had it been long. This was one reason why the pamphlet was revolutionary: its briefness and use of plain speech allowed common people to understand complex political and philosophical ideas.

Called "the first American self-help book ... for those who could not imagine life without a monarch,"[1] *Common Sense* became an instant best seller,[2] stirring opinion across the continent and, perhaps more importantly, boosting morale in the Continental army commanded by George Washington—a man who was to be the first president of the young United States.

> "The tremendous impact of Paine's writings in Europe and America has never been adequately explained, and Paine's relationship to the expansion of popular participation in politics—a major achievement in the Age of Revolution—is still not clear."
>
> Eric Foner, *Tom Paine and Revolutionary America*

Approach

Paine rejected the notion that reconciliation with Great Britain was possible, even if some still desired it. Two aspects of Paine's response to those who opposed independence are noteworthy.

First, he drew from Enlightenment thinkers who believed that political systems should be based on reason, not tradition. Second, he knew a great deal about contemporary American politics and was able to apply Enlightenment ideas clearly to them. Paine's innovation was to ask not *if* the colonies should become independent, but *how*. In his view, continued British rule was not an option.

While most political philosophers had to create hypothetical examples of how their ideas might work, Paine was able to draw upon real-world events that were already unpopular, such as the Coercive Acts*—laws imposed by the British government on the state of Massachusetts and intended to punish the colonists for behavior considered to be insubordinate (that is, rebellious). His ideas were therefore not abstract; they were applicable to current affairs.

While thinkers in Europe were asking questions about what rights people should be allowed, Paine pointed to those that were already being denied or abused. This combination of an intellectual analysis and an appeal to emotion struck a chord with readers from all over the continent.

Contribution in Context

Paine was the inheritor of an eclectic set of ideas originated by figures such as the Genevan Enlightenment philosopher Jean-Jacques Rousseau,* "a man much esteemed by Paine,"[3] who had already argued that democracy was the best form of government. Rousseau had developed his thinking by studying the British political philosophers John Locke* and Thomas Hobbes.* The historian Christopher Hitchens* points out that it is "not known whether Paine ever read Hobbes, and he always denied having read John Locke's essay on *Civil Government*,"[4] but we can still see their influences in *Common Sense*.

Paine was able to apply these ideas directly to the plight of the colonies; in this way, he was not only critiquing British misrule but also the British political system. Unlike Locke and Hobbes, Paine rejected the idea of a king—even one limited by a constitution—and opted instead for a system that called for leaders to be chosen and removed from office on a regular basis.

It is difficult to know exactly where to position Paine within academic thought. In *Common Sense*, the stance he takes against monarchy allows us to identify him as a republican,* and his emphasis on equality, freedom, and individual rights suggests that he was a liberal* and a radical.* However, it is only by examining his later works, such as *The Rights of Man** (1791), that we can definitively say that he was influenced by social contract theory.* In *The Rights of Man*, Paine applied existing political theory to the events that had led to the American crisis,and later to the French Revolution.* More importantly, he adapted and combined ideas from multiple sources that fit his vision of freedom.

---

1. Craig Nelson, *Thomas Paine: His Life, His Time and the Birth of Modern Nations* (London: Profile Books, 2007), 84.
2. Thomas Paine, *The Thomas Paine Reader*, ed. Michael Foot and Isaac Kramnick (London: Penguin, 1987), 10.
3. Christopher Hitchens, *Thomas Paine's Rights of Man* (New York: Grove Press, 2006), 95.
4. Hitchens, *Rights of Man*, 106.

SECTION 2
IDEAS

MAIN IDEAS

KEY POINTS

* *Common Sense* argued that Britain had betrayed its colonies, and that America was morally required to fight for independence.
* Paine showed that the grievances Americans felt toward Britain represented a larger social injustice.
* He wrote in a bold, dramatic style, and persuaded his audience using language they were familiar with.

Key Themes

Common Sense's argument is built on the premise that government "even in its best state is but a necessary evil,"[1] and at its worst is an "intolerable one." As such, Paine begins by describing how governments, in particular monarchies, can be harmful. He argues that American independence is inevitable and insists that without it, British tyranny would continue to cause social injustice. He ties these ideas together by touching upon a philosophical concept that was important to Enlightenment* thinkers: an examination of the "state of nature"* (that is, the hypothetical way in which people would have lived before societies were formed).

Paine's explanation of the social contract*—an idea based on the assumption that human nature is governed by reason, and that people should only trade so many rights for stable government—is subtle.

First, he asks the reader to imagine each person living on his or her own, in a "state of nature." It would be logical for people to want to create a "society,"[2] since, according to Paine, the "strength of one man is so unequal to his wants and his mind so unsuited to perpetual solitude."[3] In coming together, people would need to agree upon rules and choose leaders to govern them.

However, Paine writes, the invention of government had been conceived in "dark and slavish times,"[4] and was now "imperfect, subject to convulsions, and incapable of producing what it seems to promise."[5] According to Paine, examples of these "imperfections" include England's unwritten constitution (called "unwritten" because it existed in multiple documents and practices, and not as a single, unified text) and hereditary monarchy,* in which the crown was passed from generation to generation according to tradition. In particular, Paine sees the king as the source of all social injustice.

Paine accuses the British government of crimes stretching back several years. Among these crimes are unfair taxation, lack of representation in the British Parliament, and the bloody battles of Lexington and Concord* and Bunker Hill in 1775, when the Revolutionary army engaged the British army in the colony of Massachusetts, with great loss of life.

In Paine's view, reconciliation would not resolve the colonists' grievances because it would not change the fact that the colonies were ruled by a king. As such, Paine charges those who support reconciliation with "opening a door to eternal tyranny."[6] And because Britain had refused to agree to colonial demands, the only two options Paine allows for are surrender or revolution. From this perspective, war seems inevitable: the colonists' position was intolerable and would not change unless they escaped British rule.

> "Society in every state is a blessing but government even in its best state is but a necessary evil; in its worst state an intolerable one."
>
> Thomas Paine, *Common Sense*

Exploring the Ideas

Paine doesn't just disapprove of the British government's policies. He writes that the very system is corrupt. He denounces the hereditary monarchy as "an insult and an imposition on prosperity,"[7] and reasons that the way to correct the problem is to change the system. This, in Paine's view, is why Americans must become independent: there was no will in Britain to change from a constitutional monarchy,* which they saw as a liberal, workable system.

America would have to break from the mother country herself. Paine writes that the Old World is "overrun with oppression," and freedom has been "hunted from the globe."[8] Paine believed that no amount of negotiation with Britain would change this. It would therefore be necessary to construct a new political system based in part on the beliefs of Enlightenment thinkers such as Thomas Hobbes,* John Locke,* Jean-Jacques Rousseau,* and the Dutch philosopher Hugo Grotius,* who was among the first to introduce the idea of natural individual rights in the seventeenth century.

In asking readers to consider what a state of nature might look like, Paine also asks them to reevaluate the social norms with which they had been raised. Paine claims to draw his form of government from "a principle of nature."[9] He also argues that the state of nature proves that hereditary monarchy is illogical—or, as he put it, turns it "into ridicule by giving mankind an ass for a lion."[10] Furthermore, Paine insists that "men, who look upon themselves [as] born to reign and others to obey, soon grow insolent." For Paine, the logic is clear: there are no kings in nature, and "there should be none in society."[11]

Language and Expression

The key ideas in *Common Sense* are best understood as a series of arguments and counterarguments designed to inspire the public to support revolution. Paine begins by rejecting the idea that government should serve any interest other than that of the people. He is especially critical of hereditary monarchy, especially in the ways it limits individual rights. After citing a series of examples to show that the Bible does not support the idea of kings, Paine launches an all-out attack on British rule, citing the absurdity of an island ruling a continent, let alone much of the world.

Paine's outrage is tempered by his calm, logical support for inalienable, or guaranteed, human rights. By both illustrating the injustice of British rule and highlighting the economic practicality of war, Paine's argument addresses specific colonial concerns while also giving voice to the growing anger that colonists felt at the time.

Paine wrote in dramatic, emotional, and provocative English. He wanted the contemporary reader to understand easily why the colonies should fight for independence from Britain. If the text is difficult to read today, it is because it was written nearly 250 years ago: Paine was not writing for future generations, and modern readers may not be familiar with the political affairs of his time. Still, in arguing for how much power government should have over individuals, he speaks to a political debate still relevant to readers today.

---

1. Thomas Paine, *Common Sense* (New York: Dover Publications Inc., 1997), 3.

2. Paine, *Common Sense*, 3.

3. Paine, *Common Sense*, 3.

4. Paine, *Common Sense*, 5.

5. Paine, *Common Sense*, 5.

6. Paine, *Common Sense*, 32.

7. Paine, *Common Sense*, 12.

8. Paine, *Common Sense*, 33.

9. Paine, *Common Sense*, 5.

10. Paine, *Common Sense*, 12.

11. Paine, *Common Sense*, 33.

MODULE 6
SECONDARY IDEAS

KEY POINTS

* *Common Sense* also suggested that the colonies could both win and profit by the war.
* Paine's argument allowed Americans to question their loyalty to the British king.
* Not all the claims Paine made in *Common Sense* were realistic.

Other Ideas

Although Thomas Paine's primary goal in *Common Sense* is to convince colonists that independence is the best course of action, he makes a number of other important points. He articulates some of the perceived crimes committed under British rule and discusses the current state of the colonies—particularly their military strength.

Readers should be aware that Paine was not writing a textbook and did not feel the need to give details or evidence. For example, Paine refers to the "Massacre at Lexington," without explaining that he is referring to fighting that began in the towns of Lexington and Concord,* Massachusetts, after the British army attempted to destroy colonial military supplies.[1] Similarly, he writes,"Thousands of lives are already ruined by British barbarity,"[2] without mentioning specific incidents.

Paine understood that war with Britain would be expensive and risky, and speaks to these fears. He notes that the colonies were free from debt, and therefore prepared to "repel the forces of all the world."[3] He also said that since America possessed the "largest body of armed and disciplined men of any power under Heaven,"[4] the colonies could not afford to balk at challenging Britain on purely economical grounds. Britain's strength was its navy, which Paine describes as "formidable," though dismisses, saying "not a tenth part of them are at any one time fit for service."[5] And while the colonies had no warships of their own, Paine was confident that no country was "so happily situated, or so internally capable of raising a fleet as America."[6]

Such ideas were speculative, but also exaggerated. It was true that the British navy was in considerable disarray, but the idea that America could raise a fleet to compete with it was absurd. Readers should also note that war between Britain and the colonies would mostly mean fighting on land, so Paine's claims that America could raise a fleet to repel the British navy ultimately did not matter.

> *"Through this new language, he communicated a new vision—a utopian image of an egalitarian society—and in so doing ideas surrounding natural rights and republicanism became instantly accessible to all."*
>
> Eric Foner, *Tom Paine and Revolutionary America*

Exploring the Ideas

While America's successful revolution vindicated Paine's insistence that the colonists need "fear no external enemy,"[7] some of the claims he made were questionable. Paine seems at times more concerned with using dramatic, inflammatory language to incite colonists to support war than with making reasonable points.

For example, his analysis of colonial military capabilities can only be explained as ignorance, reckless overconfidence, or an outright lie. While it is true that the British navy was not able to blockade the entire coast, and that punitive attacks, like the burning of Falmouth,* Massachusetts, were annoyances, the reality was that in 1776 the American navy was practically nonexistent.[8] It was not until 1778, when France, Spain, and the Netherlands entered the war on America's behalf, that British naval superiority was contested.

Paine also avoided describing the specific events he cites as evidence of British tyranny, such as the battles at Lexington and Concord.* Instead, he uses broad sweeping statements to critique Britain. England's constitution, which was not a single document but a group of documents and policies, was fit only for "dark and slavish times;"[9] King George III* was the descendent of a "French Bastard;"[10] and, more importantly, Britain had heaped unforgivable injuries upon the colonies.

Overlooked

Towards the end of *Common Sense*, Paine focuses his arguments on the Quakers.* He does this for two reasons. First, Paine's father was a Quaker (though his mother was not), and this connection gave him insight into the group's opinions. Second, and more importantly, Paine was living and writing in Philadelphia, where there were many Quakers, and it was logical to ask for their support. Paine may not have anticipated that *Common Sense* would be read so widely.

In this part of the pamphlet, Paine adopts a more diplomatic tone, insisting that "our plan is for peace forever. We are tired of contention with Britain and can see no real end to it but separation."[11]

Paine knew that the Quaker religion was based on pacifism,* or opposition to war and violence. Though Quakers initially supported resistance to Britain—they had, for example, opposed the crown's taxation policies—they were alarmed by the escalating violence on both sides. Events such as the Boston Tea Party* (a political protest in the course of which activists threw a shipload of tea into Boston harbor in protest at taxes Americans were obliged to pay without representation in the British Parliament) and the passage of the Coercive Acts* (punitive laws imposed by Britain in retaliation for American rebelliousness) suggested that war was inevitable. Paine didn't think that Quakers would support war with Britain, which is why he addressed them directly—but he believed that, while they would not bear arms, that did not mean that they were required to remain neutral.

---

1. Thomas Paine, *Common Sense* (New York: Dover Publications Inc., 1997), 26.

2. Paine, *Common Sense*, 26.

3. Paine, *Common Sense,* 34.

4. Paine, *Common Sense,* 34.

5. Paine, *Common Sense,* 38.

6. Paine, *Common Sense,* 36.

7. Paine, *Common Sense*, 39.

8. Stephen Howarth, *To Shining Sea: A History of the United States Navy, 1775–1998* (Norman: University of Oklahoma Press, 1991), 6.

9. Paine, *Common Sense,* 5.

10. Paine, *Common Sense,* 33.

11. Paine, *Common Sense,* 53.

MODULE 7
ACHIEVEMENT

KEY POINTS

* Paine's pamphlet convinced many Americans to favor independence.
* *Common Sense* was written to inflame public opinion.
* Paine played less of a role in shaping the United States than in helping it achieve independence.

Assessing the Argument

It is clear that in *Common Sense* Thomas Paine wanted to inspire the colonial masses to support and fight for independence. As such, Paine maintains an outraged and incendiary tone throughout. In addition, he employs two broad tactics to persuade his audience. First, Paine uses economic, moral, and theological evidence to justify his position. Second, he uses these same types of evidence to refute arguments against independence.

It is unclear, however, how much Paine hoped to influence events after the American Revolution.* *Common Sense* certainly does not offer a full, coherent plan for creating a system of government. Paine does suggest some specifics, such as term limits for government officials and presidential elections, but we cannot be sure if he meant these as a blueprint, or if he simply wanted to show colonists that there were alternatives to hereditary monarchies.*

Ultimately, Paine did not contribute directly to the form of the United States government. Nevertheless, he achieved his primary goal when the colonies won their revolution. Paine's claims that the colonies would succeed in their war made him seem prophetic.

> "We have it in our power to begin the world over again."
>
> Thomas Paine, *Common Sense*

Achievement in Context

The success of *Common Sense* must be seen as connected to the success of the American Revolutionary War. More, it was written and structured according to what Paine thought would persuade the average colonist. We should also note that Paine's text was directly linked to the events of the crisis in the American colonies, and it probably would not have been published under different circumstances.

Paine's fame lasted because of the colonial victory. Having inspired public support for revolution, Paine did not stop writing about his ideas.Although he addressed the specific situation in America, he also believed his vision was universal, arguing that it was within America's power to "begin the world over again."[1] And indeed, the Revolution that he helped inspire was a major historical event; it contributed, for example, to the French Revolution* that began shortly after, in 1789.

Paine's pamphlet also interested academics, particularly those who studied theology. For example, *Common Sense* attacks the idea that monarchs were divinely appointed. In France, the attack on hereditary monarchy had literal consequences in the execution of the French king, Louis XVI,* in 1793. Similarly, the separation of religion and politics, a foundation of the new American government, has since become important throughout the Western world.

Common Sense is also one of the cornerstones of American political literature. Paine's fiery prose style set the tone for the American Revolution, and for future American political writers. He continued to write this way in his later pamphlets, such as *The American Crises.* He was "aware that he was creating a new style of writing,"[2] and that "most writers in the eighteenth century believed that to write for a mass audience meant to sacrifice refinement for coarseness and triviality."[3] *Common Sense*'s success showed that this was not true.

Limitations

Paine's contemporaries, such as the US's second president, John Adams,* expressed outrage that "history is to ascribe the American Revolution to Thomas Paine,"[4] and attributed more influence to the likes of the political activist Joseph Hewes,* an important signatory of the Declaration of Independence.* *Common Sense* should nevertheless be viewed as a work of immense importance— both for its role in political change, and for its influence on political writing.

Over time, the ideas in *Common Sense* spread. Paine's thinking found its way into both the Declaration of Independence and the US Constitution,* documents on which the history of the United States as an independent and free nation are instituted.

More importantly, Paine's ideas endured beyond the Revolution, both because Enlightenment* principles were becoming widely accepted, and because Paine's writing style was so accessible.

Prior to *Common Sense*'s publication in 1776, political writing was mainly directed toward the intellectual elite. Paine's style changed that. According to the University of Virginia professor of history Sophia Rosenfeld,* the effectiveness of "common sense" as a political weapon could be "measured by its many opposition imitators, who seized upon the form's commercial as well as polemical potential."[5] That is, we can see that Paine's style was influential because it had many imitators who valued it as a tool for communicating with the general public. Paine's style became a "commonplace polemical tool in a bitterly fought struggle over the future of politics"[6] because, politicians learned, the language in which a message was delivered was as important as the message itself—perhaps more so.

Thus Paine's text began a new tradition in writing about politics. As the Australian political theorist John Keane* points out, democratic revolution required a "prior democratic revolution in prose."[7] Paine's use of plain language would later be used to great effect in political speeches, such as those of Franklin D. Roosevelt,* who served as president of the United States from 1933 to 1945. Roosevelt channeled Paine when he affirmed "the nation's commitment to defeat fascism and make freedom universal."[8] In saying "make freedom universal," Roosevelt reminded Americans of their heritage.

Paine's belief that America's cause was the world's cause, and that freedom and justice were universal principles, has become part of the American psyche, and Roosevelt used this to influence his audience. Thus we can see that *Common Sense* has had a lasting impact on American political expression from speechwriting to propaganda.

---

1. Thomas Paine, *Common Sense* (New York: Dover Publications Inc., 1997), 51.

2. Eric Foner, *Tom Paine and Revolutionary America* (London, New York, and Oxford: Oxford University Press, 1976), 85.

3. Foner, *Tom Paine and Revolutionary America*, 85.

4. John Adams, *To Thomas Jefferson, vol. 10* of *The Works of John Adams, Second President of the United States: With a Life of the Author, Notes and Illustrations, by His Grandson Charles Francis Adams* (Boston: Little, Brown, 1856), accessed September 22, 2013, http://oll.libertyfund.org/title/2127/193637/3103690.

5. Sophia Rosenfeld, *Common Sense: A Political History* (Cambridge, MA: Harvard University Press, 2011), 44.

6. Rosenfeld, *Common Sense, 54.*

7. John Keane, *Tom Paine: A Political Life* (London, New York, and Berlin: Bloomsbury, 2009), 295.

8. Roosevelt quoted in Harvey J. Kaye, *Thomas Paine and the Promise of America* (New York: Hill & Wang, 2005), 195.

PLACE IN THE AUTHOR'S WORK

KEY POINTS

* Paine believed that man had certain natural rights,* and that God did not interfere with humanity.

* *Common Sense* includes Paine's philosophical views—but its purpose is to convince America to go to war.

* The text made Paine a celebrity and cemented his role in American history.

Positioning

Common Sense was Thomas Paine's first significant work. His earlier political writing, such as the 1772 pamphlet *The Case of the Officers of Excise*,[1] was more limited in scope, and perhaps produced out of self-interest. The essay "Observations on the Military Character of Ants"—a satire in which red ants, symbolizing the British army, deprived brown ants of their natural rights—appeared in the July 1775 issue of the *Pennsylvania Magazine*. Paine used a pseudonym, Curioso,[2] because of libel laws,* which made it illegal to criticize the government or to incite contempt for the monarch. For the same reason, *Common Sense* was initially published anonymously, though it did not take long for its author to be identified. It is difficult to overstate how important the pamphlet was to Paine's career; it "burst from the press with an effect which has rarely been produced by types and paper in any age or country,"[3] and Paine became a celebrity.

Common Sense was written as a call to arms. The battles of

Lexington and Concord* (April 1775) and Bunker Hill (June 1775) had already taken place by the time it was published in January 1776, and the point of no return occurred only five months after, when the Declaration of Independence* was signed. Between 1773 and 1776, Paine wrote 16 pamphlets collectively titled *The American Crises*. Written in a similar style to *Common Sense*, they were designed to improve colonial morale and spread Paine's philosophical ideas.

> *"Paine's work burst from the press with an effect which has rarely been produced by types and paper in any age or country."*
>
> Moncure Daniel Conway, *The Life of Thomas Paine*

Integration

Common Sense was instrumental in gaining public support for the Revolution.* It also established Paine's reputation and helped popularize his later works, in which he explained his ideas more thoroughly.

These later texts affirmed his unwavering stance against monarchies and his commitment to liberty. He remained a liberal* (in the sense of one committed to equality and regular elections) and a deist,* believing that a faith in God should be founded on reason rather than tradition. He would expand upon these and many other ideas in his seminal work *The Rights of Man* (1791). The book became popular because of Paine's reputation, and it is considered his most important contribution to political philosophy.

Significance

Though *Common Sense* made Paine a celebrity, it did not contain fully articulated versions of Paine's ideas. Paine's later works were true academic texts and influential in their own right, though readers should note that their publication was only guaranteed by the success of *Common Sense*. Paine's pamphlet took on historical significance because America had won its independence and created a government based on the liberal principles he had written about; his later works built on this reputation.

Paine wrote *The Rights of Man* because he was inspired by the French Revolution,* during which the French monarch, Louis XVI,* was executed and several constitutions were drafted. In it, Paine attacks hereditary succession and a monarchy whose "despotism resident in the person of the King divides and subdivides itself into a thousand shapes and forms."[4] His other important text, *The Age of Reason* (1794), is primarily concerned with religion and makes an argument for deism. This was a departure from his other works in that it risked religious controversy. By comparison, where *Common Sense* contained religious sentiments, these were only to justify the war for independence. It should be noted that these ideas were an extension of Enlightenment thinking; they were not Paine's originally.

---

1. Thomas Paine, *The Writings of Thomas Paine*, vol. 4, ed. Moncure Daniel Conway (New York: G.P. Putnam and Sons, 1894).

2. Edward Larkin, "Inventing an American Public: Thomas Paine, the *Pennsylvania Magazine*, and American Revolutionary Discourse," *Early American Literature* 33, no. 3 (1998): 250–76.

3. Moncure Daniel Conway, *The Life of Thomas Paine: With a History of His Literary, Political and Religious Career in America, France, and England; to Which Is Added a Sketch of Paine by William Cobbett,* vol. 1 (New York and London: G.P. Putnam and Sons, 1894), 25.

4. Thomas Paine, *The Rights of Man* (New York: Dover Publications Inc., 1999), 14.

SECTION 3
IMPACT

THE FIRST RESPONSES

KEY POINTS

- Contemporaries criticized *Common Sense* for its superficial arguments and provocative style.

- Candidus,* a writer who believed that the colonies should remain loyal to Britain, argued that the rebels would be more tyrannical than the king.

- Even those who agreed with Paine that the colonies should become independent did not always agree about the form the new government should take.

Criticism

The primary critics of Thomas Paine's *Common Sense* were loyalists,* colonials who wanted to remain part of the British Empire. They saw the pamphlet as a dangerous work composed by "a writer whose powerful literary style was crucial to disseminating its irrational and dangerous arguments."[1] Loyalists often wrote that conditions in the society Paine envisioned would be worse, and that the rebels would be more ruthless than the British. For example, a writer who used the pseudonym Candidus*—a man historians believe to be the Scottish-born military officer James Chalmers—warned that if the colonials won the war against the British, they would persecute the loyalists with "more unrelenting virulence than the professed advocates of arbitrary power."[2]

Loyalist critics such as the poet Jonathan Odell from New

Jersey came from a variety of social backgrounds,[3] and were united by political views that cut across social and geographical divides. Their arguments, however, had little impact on the American Revolution;* the colonies declared their independence soon after *Common Sense* was published, just as Paine insisted they must, and the loyalist position rapidly became shaky.

> "[Common Sense *is]* a poor, ignorant, malicious, short-sighted, crapulous mass."
>
> John Adams, *The Works of John Adams*

Responses

The second edition of *Common Sense* was published in February 1776. In it, Paine addresses his critics directly. He claims that he delayed publication of the new edition because he was waiting for a "refutation of the doctrine of Independence,"[4] but that "no answer hath yet appeared."[5] This shows the contempt he felt for his critics' position.

Paine did not respond to critics by name or focus on specific disagreements. However, we can guess from his writing which criticisms he felt needed to be answered. For example, he responded to critiques of his anonymity by saying, "who the author of this production is, is wholly unnecessary,"[6] and, because he took accusations of partisanship seriously, he insisted that he was "unconnected with any party and under no sort of influence public or private."[7]

Paine was also critiqued for the alternatives to monarchy he offered. Paine argued that monarchy had "laid the world in 'blood and ashes',"[8] and he felt a similar contempt for England's unwritten constitution. However, critics attacked his alternative, a form of republicanism,* in which all citizens had a say in government. First, they noted that it had already been attempted in the "Protectorate"* of the English revolutionary general and political leader Oliver Cromwell* in the period between 1649 and 1658 when England was a republic. Loyalists also pointed out that Cromwell had himself become a tyrant.

Second, according to John Adams,* Paine's system was no better than a monarchy because it preserved power "in a single sovereign body."[9] Adams, who would become the second president of the United States, agreed with the "necessity of independence and America's ability to maintain it,"[10] but disagreed about what form the new nation's government should take. He dismissed Paine's idea of a direct assembly, in which all people had a say in laws that were passed, as unworkable.[11]

Conflict and Consensus

Since its purpose had been to call for revolution, there was no need for a third edition of *Common Sense* after the war began in earnest. We can therefore only understand the later criticisms of the text based on which of its suggestions were rejected when the new government was formed. Though Paine's vision did resemble what was eventually created, many of his ideas were significantly altered.

Adams—who later referred to *Common Sense* as a "poor,

ignorant, malicious, short-sighted, crapulous mass"[12]—felt that "whether Paine knew it or not, his stubborn appeal to undivided popular sovereignty helped to drag republican politics a few yards towards democracy."[13] Adams saw himself as "keeping apart the conflicting ideas of republicanism and democracy,"[14] and he believed that Paine's popular sovereignty, or system in which all citizens had a say in government, was a radical and dangerous idea. Adams believed that all forms of government, not just hereditary monarchies,* were apt to abuse power, and that Paine had "forgotten the elementary truth that democracy dangerously concentrates power in the hands of the many."[15] Ultimately, Adams was a central figure in the structure of the new American government, and his opinion carried significant weight.

1. Philip Gould, *Writing the Rebellion: Loyalists and the Literature of Politics in British America* (New York: Oxford University Press, 2013), 121.

2. James Chalmers, *Plain Truth: Addressed to the Inhabitants of America, Containing, Remarks on a Late Pamphlet, Entitled Common Sense* (Charleston, SC: Nabu Press, 2014).

3. Cynthia Dublin Edelberg, *Jonathan Odell: The Loyalist Poet of the American Revolution* (Durham, NC: Duke University Press, 1987).

4. Thomas Paine, *Common Sense* (New York: Dover Publications Inc., 1997), 2.

5. Paine, *Common Sense,* 2.

6. Paine, *Common Sense,* 2.

7. Paine, *Common Sense,* 2

8. Paine, *Common Sense,* 16.

9. John Adams quoted in John Keane, *Tom Paine: A Political Life* (London, New York, and Berlin: Bloomsbury, 2009), 125.

10. Keane, *Tom Paine,* 125.

11. Keane, *Tom Paine,* 125.

12. John Adams, *To Thomas Jefferson*, vol. 10 of *The Works of John Adams, Second President of the United States: With a Life of the Author, Notes and Illustrations, by His Grandson Charles Francis Adams* (Boston: Little Brown, 1856), accessed September 22, 2013, http://oll.libertyfund.org/title/2127/193637/3103690.

13. See Keane, *Tom Paine*, 127.

14. Keane, *Tom Paine*, 126.

15. Keane, *Tom Paine*, 131.

MODULE 10
THE EVOLVING DEBATE

KEY POINTS

- *Common Sense* revolutionized political prose and shaped politics both in the colonies and beyond.
- The pamphlet drew from Enlightenment* philosophical principles.
- The text's focus on individual rights means it is relevant to American political debate today.

Uses and Problems

Thomas Paine drew his ideas from a mix of Enlightenment political theories, especially those that dealt with social contract theory.* Although these ideas had been purely theoretical up to this point, the American Revolutionary War* put them to the test. The most crucial and progressive aspect of Paine's pamphlet was that it took prior thought and used it to inform social and political change.

In short, Paine's pamphlet argued that important Enlightenment ideas were not just abstractions, but key tools informing government.

It is no coincidence that the French Revolution* began in 1789, only six years after the American Revolution ended. The social upheaval in France was informed by the same philosophers that Paine drew from in *Common Sense*, and by the real events in North America, where the newly independent United States had formed a republic (a system based on the idea that nations do not need to be governed by monarchs).

The republic, free of kings and hereditary monarchy,* was perhaps the most powerful idea in *Common Sense*, and Paine expanded upon it in *The Rights of Man* (1791). It is a system that continues to find expression in today's liberal democracies. That said, the formation of republics is not always free of trouble or resistance. For example, Edmund Burke,* a member of the British Parliament and critic of British colonial policy, was initially a supporter of the French Revolution but soon became horrified by the bloodshed. He rejected notions of natural rights, asking, "Am I to congratulate a highway man and murderer who has broke prison upon the recovery of his natural rights?"[1]

> *"Men of all ranks have embarked in the controversy, from different motives, and with various designs; but all have been ineffectual and the period of debate is closed. Arms, as the last resource, decide the contest."*
>
> Thomas Paine, *Common Sense*

Schools of Thought

Many of Paine's foundational ideas were borrowed. We have already encountered some of those who originated the important ideas in *Common Sense*, such as the political philosophers Thomas Hobbes,* John Locke,* and Jean-Jacques Rousseau.* Paine's focus on social contract theory, in which people give up some individual rights in order to form a just society, also associates him with thinkers who came later. One such example is Pierre-Joseph Proudhon,* a French politician and liberal social theorist.

Proudhon founded a philosophy called mutualism, which is based on the idea that societies function best when people depend upon one another. Another descendent of the social contract theory school of thought was American political philosopher John Rawls.* Rawls's *A Theory of Justice* (1971) was a controversial but critically acclaimed book about how resources should best be distributed in a society.

It is important to note that *Common Sense* had little effect on the philosophical and academic conversation surrounding social contract theory. It was not, however, intended to: it was *The Rights of Man* that indicated Paine's importance as a political theorist. A more thorough description of Paine's beliefs, *The Rights of Man* "indicates [Paine's] importance in forcing a broadening of the political nation and the democratizing of national politics."[2]

The most important idea in this book is how Paine defines natural rights—that is, rights that are so fundamental that they cannot even be made law (since that would imply that they could be taken away). The emergence of the American nation helped put these ideas into practice and encouraged other societies to model themselves on the social contract.

In Current Scholarship

Today's political scholars recognize Paine's *Common Sense* as a landmark in American and world history. For example, Harvey Kaye,* a political scientist at the University of Wisconsin, writes that Paine "emboldened Americans to turn their colonial rebellion into a revolutionary war, defined the new nation in a democratically expansive and progressive fashion, and articulated an American identity charged with exceptional purpose and promise."[3] Today, Paine's ideas seem so central to our beliefs about justice and individual rights that it is "almost impossible to understand his ideas as the revolution in thinking that they once were."[4]

The Enlightenment ideas that Paine drew on have significantly influenced Western politics, cultures, and governments. By the end of the Cold War*—a period of tension between the United States and the Soviet Union from 1947 to 1991—the world was experiencing what American political scientist Francis Fukuyama* has described as a "liberal revolution"—one that "has broken out of its original beachheads in Western Europe and North America."[5]

The liberalism* that Fukuyama refers to, while not universal, has certainly become widespread in the Western world, and it reflects Paine's ideas about liberty and government. Few Western countries maintain their hereditary monarchies, and where they have (for example, the United Kingdom), the monarch has been stripped of power. Today, scholars study *Common Sense* to learn about its role in the American Revolutionary War and its effect on political speech and writing.

1. Edmund Burke, *Reflections on the Revolution in France* (Oxford: Oxford University Press, 2006), 8.
2. Mark Philip, Introduction to *Rights of Man, Common Sense, and Other Political Writings*, by Thomas Paine (Oxford: Oxford University Press. 2008), xxiii.
3. Harvey J. Kaye, *Thomas Paine and the Promise of America* (New York: Hill & Wang, 2005), 4.
4. Craig Nelson, *Thomas Paine: His Life, His Time and the Birth of Modern Nations* (London: Profile Books, 2007), 10.
5. Francis Fukuyama, *The End of History and the Last Man* (London: Penguin, 2012), 50.

IMPACT AND INFLUENCE TODAY

KEY POINTS

* *Common Sense* is a landmark in the history of the American Revolutionary War.*
* Although radical for its time, *Common Sense*'s core ideas now seem ordinary.
* Paine's arguments are still relevant today in that governments continue to exert power over their citizens.

Position

Today, Thomas Paine's *Common Sense* is best seen as a historical document. It tells us about the ideas and events that were controversial in 1775, and it also shows us how Enlightenment* principles such as natural rights* informed eighteenth-century political thought. For Paine, tyranny stood in the way of natural rights, and these rights were enshrined in his vision of a free and democratic American state.

The text is also part of the narrative of the American Revolution, and students of history can see how it contributed to the country's formation. Paine played an important role in this narrative, and the text is interesting because of what it can tell us about political writing and propaganda. Additionally, we can see how Paine's ideas are still relevant to today's liberal* democracies. That said, although *Common Sense* is directly related to modern liberal democratic thought, it has been less influential than Paine's later works, particularly *The Rights of Man** (1791).

"The impact of ... Common Sense *as a political weapon can also be measured by its many Opposition imitators, who seized upon the form's commercial as well as polemical potential."*

Sophia Rosenfeld, *Common Sense: A Political History*

Interaction

Common Sense's contribution to eighteenth-century political thought was limited in two ways. First, Paine wrote to inflame public support for independence, not to influence philosophical debate. Additionally, the Declaration of Independence* was signed only a few months after the pamphlet was published; from that point, there was no turning back from war, making much of Paine's argument, therefore, moot.

Second, though Paine was on the "right side of history," the "worldwide liberal revolution" described by the American political theorist Francis Fukuyama* was still several centuries away.[1] It was not until the twentieth century that government by hereditary monarchy* fell out of favor. Similarly, Paine's writing did not have much immediate effect on imperialism*— in which countries exerted power and influence over other countries through diplomacy or military force—though it was one of the grounds on which he critiqued British rule.

That said, Paine's world view ultimately endured. Today's liberal democracies generally allow for the natural rights of man to coexist peacefully with the government at large—an idea true to the spirit of *Common Sense*. In the twenty-first century, few are comfortable with the idea of one nation dominating another, refusing it any representation, and imposing unfair taxes. Additionally, not many people support a return to pre-democratic government. Intellectuals today who entertain such a possibility remain at the fringes of serious academic debate or are considered political extremists. Thus Paine's legacy is reflected in the forms of government that are most common today.

The Continuing Debate

The debate about individual rights continues to evolve today. The Western world has come to revile the idea of a nation that does not guarantee the natural rights of its citizens. One explanation for this is what the French cultural theorist Paul Virilio* calls ideological contamination,* in which new technologies allow ideas to spread faster and further. This is one reason why Western intellectual movements, such as those informed by the Enlightenment, have become so widely appealing.[2]

---

1. Francis Fukuyama, *The End of History and the Last Man* (London: Penguin, 2012), 39.
2. Paul Virilio, *The Information Bomb*, trans. Chris Turner (London: Verso, 2005), 15.

MODULE 12
WHERE NEXT?

KEY POINTS

* Paine's text remains central to understanding the American Revolution* and is still studied for its dramatic, inflammatory prose.
* *Common Sense* will continue to be seen as one of the main inspirations for American independence.
* *Common Sense* is required reading for those who wish to understand why America went to war with Britain.

Potential

Thomas Paine's *Common Sense* is likely to remain an important and influential text in the future. Although it was not a great philosophical work, its role in inspiring support for independence from Great Britain makes it significant. Furthermore, because *Common Sense* was so widely read, Paine deserves credit for popularizing key Enlightenment* ideas.

Paine's pamphlet is also important in that its ideas found their way into two documents that were foundational to the new United States: the Constitution* and the Declaration of Independence,* in which Thomas Jefferson,* who would become the third president of the United States, emphasized the importance of "natural rights."*

> "[Paine] emboldened Americans to turn their colonial rebellion into a revolutionary war, defined the new nation in a democratically expansive and progressive fashion, and articulated an American identity charged with exceptional purpose and promise."
>
> Harvey J. Kaye, *Thomas Paine and the Promise of America*

Future Directions

Paine's core ideas will probably not be developed further. They are no longer controversial, and much of what Paine argued for has been widely achieved: the formation of governments that allow their citizens natural rights, an end to hereditary monarchy,* free elections, and, of course, American independence. In today's liberal* democracies, these ideas fall into what the American communications expert Daniel C. Hallin* describes as the "sphere of consensus,"[1] in that they are rarely questioned.

That said, the pamphlet marks a turning point in history. Paine's plain, accessible writing style is now a common feature of political speech. As for its ideas, the fact that readers now struggle to understand why it was so controversial shows how influential Paine's ideas became; today's liberal democracies fulfill most, if not all, of *Common Sense*'s demands. *Common Sense* also resonates because of its criticism of tyrannical governments. Paine's argument for justice is inspiring, and reminds us that America's cause was, and is, a noble one.

Summary

Common Sense was different from other eighteenth-century

political texts because of its accessibility and inflammatory prose. Paine attacked any view that ran counter to his argument. He took the radical* ideas of the English Enlightenment philosopher John Locke*—that monarchs could be replaced if they broke the social contract*—and made them even more extreme. Paine heaped scorn upon the British king, George III,* ridiculed the hereditary system, and ultimately made it acceptable for his readers to disobey British rule.

Common Sense was successful not because of its intellectual achievement, but because Paine grasped what was important to the average colonist. In this sense, it was a masterpiece, and it helped spread Enlightenment principles to the masses. It is important for those who want to understand the Revolutionary War, the formation of the new American government, and how the American system eventually influenced other governments around the world. "The cause of America is in a great measure the cause of mankind,"[2] Paine argued, and, as with so many of his predictions, he was correct.

The creation of the United States has greatly influenced today's liberal democracies.

---

1. Daniel C. Hallin, *The Uncensored War: The Media and Vietnam* (Berkeley: University of California Press, 1989), 116.

2. Thomas Paine, *Common Sense* (New York: Dover Publications Inc., 1997), 2.

GLOSSARY OF TERMS

1. **American Revolutionary War (1775–83):** a military conflict between Britain and the 13 American colonies, although it eventually drew in France, Spain, and the Netherlands. Also known as the American War of Independence.

2. **Anarchy:** general disorder resulting from individuals' unwillingness to recognize authority. Some political thinkers—giving primacy to self-regulating individual freedom and dismissing the need for government—argue in favor of anarchy as a form of social organization.

3. **Boston Tea Party:** an incident on December 16, 1773, in which colonists boarded three British ships in Boston harbor and threw their consignment of tea overboard. This was in response to the Tea Act of 1773, which was part of legislation that both raised revenue and established that Britain could impose taxes on the colonies.

4. **British Empire:** a maritime—or naval—empire established between the sixteenth and eighteenth centuries. It comprised colonies and territories such as Canada, Australia, New Zealand, South Africa, India, and what would become the United States.

5. **Burning of Falmouth:** an incident in October 1775, when the British navy bombarded the town of Falmouth. Originally located in Massachusetts, the site is now a part of Maine.

6. **Coercive Acts:** nicknamed the "Intolerable Acts" by colonists in favor of revolution, these were a series of laws imposed upon Massachusetts that, among other things, placed it under the authority of leaders appointed by the British king, George III.

7. **Cold War (1947–91):** a period of tension between the United States and the Soviet Union. It did not result in war between the countries, but was instead carried out through espionage and proxy wars.

8. **Constitutional monarchy:** a form of government in which the power of the monarch is limited through the passage of a constitution.

9. **Declaration of Independence:** a statement that the 13 colonies no longer considered themselves to be part of the British Empire. The declaration was

ratified (that is, officially agreed) at the Second Continental Congress on July 4, 1776.

10. **Deism:** the belief that reason rather than tradition should be the foundation for belief in God.

11. **English liberties:** limits on the power of kings, such as the right to be tried by a jury and restrictions on the monarch's power to raise taxes.

12. **Enlightenment:** a movement in seventeenth- and eighteenth-century Europe that challenged commonly held ideas based in tradition and faith, and tried to advance knowledge through rationality and science.

13. **First Continental Congress:** a meeting from September to October 1774 that petitioned King George III for redress of grievances. It included representatives from 12 of the 13 colonies (the state of Georgia did not attend).

14. **French Revolution (1789–99):** a period of political and social upheaval that culminated in the execution of King Louis XVI and the drafting of several temporary constitutions.

15. **Grammar school:** a type of school. The grammar schools of Paine's times were privately run establishments that taught a limited range of subjects, including the Scriptures, Latin, Greek and mathematics.

16. **Hereditary monarchy:** a system of government according to which the crown is passed from one generation to the next, usually through the eldest male heir.

17. **Ideological contamination:** a process by which new technologies enable the swift spread of ideas from one location to the next.

18. **Imperialism:** a policy in which a country exerts power and influence over other countries through economic policy, diplomacy, or military force.

19. **Lexington and Concord:** two battles that occurred in April 1775 in towns near Boston. Fighting began when the British army attempted to destroy colonial military supplies and met local resistance.

20. **Libel:** a system of laws that, among other things, made it illegal to criticize the government of the day or to incite hatred or contempt of the monarch. Publishing

anonymously was a common tactic used to avoid arrest.

21. **Liberalism:** a political philosophy that emphasizes freedom, equality, and regularly contested elections.

22. **Loyalists:** a faction of colonists who wanted to remain part of the British Empire.

23. **Natural rights:** universal and absolute rights with which each individual is born, such as the right to "the pursuit of happiness." These rights are separate from legal rights.

24. **Pacifism:** a philosophy that opposes war and violence.

25. **Polymath:** someone whose expertise spans several different fields.

26. **Presidential system:** a type of government headed by a president who is elected by the people or the people's representatives.

27. **Protectorate:** period from 1649 to 1658, when England was a republic and Oliver Cromwell ruled as Lord Protector.

28. **Quakers:** a Christian denomination that originated in seventeenth-century England. Opposed to war and violence.

29. **Radicalism:** any form of progressive liberal ideology. At the time *Common Sense* was published, radicalism meant those who wanted to break from England to create a fairer society.

30. **Realpolitik:** a nineteenth-century term referring to the practical and achievable aspects of political action as opposed to action based on moral or ideological considerations.

31. **Republicanism:** an ideology that rejected the notion of hereditary monarchy.

32. ***The Rights of Man:*** Paine's 1791 book, written in response to the French Revolution, which began in 1789, and to Edmund Burke's *Reflections on the Revolutions in France*, which had been critical of the revolution. In it, Paine states that revolution is an acceptable response if the government is incapable or unwilling to guarantee certain basic or "'natural' rights."

33. **Second Continental Congress:** a meeting of colonial representatives in May

1775 to organize resistance to the British. This became the acting American government.

34. **Seven Years War (1754–63):** a war between Great Britain and France over conflicting trade interests across their respective empires.

35. **Social contract theory:** the philosophy that human nature is governed by reason, and that there is a limit to the number of rights people should give up in order to be governed.

36. **Soviet Union, or USSR (1922–91):** a federation of communist republics in northern Asia and Eastern Europe. The Union of Soviet Socialist Republics was created from the Russian Empire in the aftermath of the Russian Revolution of 1917. The Soviet Union, then the largest country in the world, became a superpower and rival to the United States during the Cold War.

37. **State of nature:** a thought experiment used by philosophers to help describe what life was like before people began to live in groups.

38. **Tea Act of 1773:** part of a series of acts designed to raise revenue and establish the principle that Britain had the right to impose taxes on the colonies. The Boston Tea Party was a response to the Tea Act.

39. **US Constitution:** the supreme legal document of the United States, ratified at the Second Continental Congress by all 13 states in 1790, it described the type of government the country would have and guaranteed each citizen certain rights and protections.

1. **John Adams (1735–1826)** was the second president of the United States and a leading advocate of independence from Britain. Though a supporter of Enlightenment principles, he was highly critical of many of Paine's ideas.

2. **Edmund Burke (1729–97)** was an Irish political theorist. He is best known for his book *Reflections on the Revolution in France*.

3. **Candidus** was the pseudonym used by the author of a 1776 pamphlet entitled *PlainTruth*. Although nobody knows for sure, the author was probably the Maryland loyalist James Chalmers.

4. **Oliver Cromwell (1599–1658)** was an English military and political leader who became the Lord Protector of England after the Civil War (1642–51). After he died, the republic collapsed, and a new king, Charles II, was offered the throne.

5. **Eric Foner (b. 1943)** is an American historian and biographer of Thomas Paine. He is best known for his work on political history.

6. **Benjamin Franklin (1706–90)** was a scientist, author, and political agitator and one of the Founding Fathers of the United States of America. He helped maintain colonial unity during the war and later served as the first ambassador of the United States to France.

7. **Francis Fukuyama (b. 1952)** is an American political scientist whose best-known work, *The End of History and the Last Man*, cites liberal democracy and free-market economics as the ultimate means for organizing society.

8. **King George III (1738–1820)** was king of Great Britain and ruler of the American colonies until the Declaration of Independence in 1776. He refused to listen to colonial demands, which ultimately led to the American Revolution.

9. **Hugo Grotius (1583–1645)** was a Dutch philosopher who introduced the idea of natural and inalienable individual rights. He helped lay the foundations of social contract theory.

10. **Daniel C. Hallin** is a researcher in media and communications at the University of San Diego. He is particularly respected for his work on how the media reflect societal norms.

11. **Joseph Hewes (1730–79)** was a Quaker from North Carolina and a signatory of the Declaration of Independence. He was also an active participant in the Continental Congress.

12. **Christopher Hitchens (1949–2011)** was a prolific writer and journalist. A self-described socialist, Hitchens took contrary views on many popular historical figures, such as Mother Theresa and Pope Benedict XVI.

13. **Thomas Hobbes (1588–1679)** was an English philosopher best remembered for his book *Leviathan*, in which he established what is now known as social contract theory. Hobbes championed government, specifically the monarchy, as the supreme defense against the chaotic "state of nature."

14. **Thomas Jefferson (1743–1826)** was an American Founding Father who was the principal author of the Declaration of Independence. He later served as the third president of the United States.

15. **Harvey J. Kaye** is the Ben & Joyce Rosenberg Professor of Democracy and Justice Studies at the University of Wisconsin. He has written two books about Thomas Paine.

16. **John Keane** is a political theorist from Australia and professor of political science at the University of Sydney and at the Wissenschaftszentrum in Berlin. His current work focuses on the Asia Pacific region.

17. **John Locke (1632–1704)** was an English philosopher and is generally regarded as the father of modern liberalism. He argued that human nature was governed by reason, and some, but not all, liberties were to be given up to the state. His best-known work, *Two Treatises of Government* (1689), is considered a landmark in political thought.

18. **King Louis XVI (1754–93)** was the king of France from 1774 to 1792. After being deposed in 1792 during a period of social unrest, he was tried and eventually executed in 1793.

19. **Jonathan Odell (1737–1818)** was a poet. Loyal to the British, he suffered legal sanctions following the Revolution.

20. **Pierre-Joseph Proudhon (1809–65)** was a French politician and liberal social

theorist.The founder of a branch of philosophy known as mutualism, he is also the first person to have declared himself an anarchist.

21. **John Rawls (1921–2002)** was an American philosopher and proponent of democracy. His most famous book, *A Theory of Justice*, was published in 1971 to critical acclaim.

22. **Franklin D. Roosevelt (1882–1945)** was the 32nd US president from 1933 until his death in 1945. He is the only president to have served four consecutive terms in office and was considered a master speaker.

23. **Sophia Rosenfeld** is a professor of history at the University of Virginia. She has done work in political discourse, linguistics, and analysis of revolutions.

24. **Jean-Jacques Rousseau (1712–78)** was a Genevan philosopher and member of the Enlightenment movement whose writings heavily influenced the French Revolution. Both *Discourse on the Origin of Inequality* and *On the Social Contract* are cornerstones of modern political thought.

25. **Paul Virilio (b. 1932)** is a French cultural theorist who philosophizes about the consequences of technology. One of his most important ideas is ideological contamination—the idea that technology leads to the free exchange of ideas between cultures.

26. **Voltaire (1694–1778)** is the pseudonym of François-Marie Arouet, a French Enlightenment writer who advocated, among other things, the rights of the individual and the separation of church and state. His 1756 work, *Essay on the Customs and the Spirit of the Nations*, influenced the way political thinkers looked at history.

27. **George Washington (1732–99)** was a veteran of the French and Indian War and became commander-in-chief of the Continental army on June 14, 1775, shortly after the battles of Lexington and Concord. He would later become the United States' first president in 1789.

 WORKS CITED

1. Adams, John. *The Works of John Adams, Second President of the United States: With a Life of the Author, Notes and Illustrations.* Boston: Little, Brown, 1856. Accessed September 22, 2013. http://oll.libertyfund.org/title/2127/193637/3103690.

2. "Thoughts on Government." Accessed November 7, 2013. http://www.constitution.org/jadams/thoughts.htm.

3. Burke, Edmund. *Reflections on the Revolution in France.* Oxford: Oxford University Press, 2006.

4. Chalmers, James. *Plain Truth: Addressed to the Inhabitants of America, Containing, Remarks on a Late Pamphlet, Entitled Common Sense.* Charleston, SC: Nabu Press, 2014.

5. Conway, Moncure Daniel. *The Life of Thomas Paine: With a History of His Literary, Political and Religious Career in America, France, and England; to Which Is Added a Sketch of Paine by William Cobbett.* New York and London: G.P. Putnam and Sons, 1894.

6. Edelberg, Cynthia Dubin. *Jonathan Odell: The Loyalist Poet of the American Revolution.* Durham, NC: Duke University Press, 1987.

7. Foner, Eric. *Tom Paine and Revolutionary America.* London, New York, and Oxford: Oxford University Press, 1976.

8. Fukuyama, Francis. *The End of History and the Last Man.* London: Penguin, 2012.

9. Gould, Philip. *Writing the Rebellion: Loyalists and the Literature of Politics in British America.* New York: Oxford University Press, 2013.

10. Hallin, Daniel C. *The Uncensored War: The Media and Vietnam.* Berkeley: University of California Press, 1989.

11. Hitchens, Christopher. *Thomas Paine's Rights of Man.* New York: Grove Press, 2006.

12. Hobbes, Thomas. *Leviathan.* Edited by J.C.A. Gaskin. Oxford and New York: Oxford University Press, 2008.

13. Howarth, Stephen. *To Shining Sea: A History of the United States Navy, 1775–1998*. Norman: University of Oklahoma Press, 1991.

14. Jefferson, Thomas. *To Thomas Paine Philadelphia, June 19, 1792*. Accessed December 8, 2014, http://www.let.rug.nl/usa/presidents/thomas-jefferson/letters-of-thomas-jefferson/jefl99.php.

15. Kaye, Harvey J. *Thomas Paine and the Promise of America*. New York: Hill & Wang, 2005.

16. Keane, John. *Tom Paine: A Political Life*. London, New York, and Berlin: Bloomsbury, 2009.

17. Larkin, Edward. "Inventing an American Public: Thomas Paine, the *Pennsylvania Magazine*, and American Revolutionary Discourse." *Early American Literature* 33, no. 3 (1998): 250–76.

18. Locke, John. *Two Treatises of Government*. Edited by Peter Laslett. Cambridge: Cambridge University Press, 1988.

19. Meacham, Jon. *Thomas Jefferson: The Art of Power*. New York: Random House Trade Paperbacks; reprint edition, 2013.

20. Nelson, Craig. *Thomas Paine: His Life, His Time and the Birth of Modern Nations*. London: Profile Books, 2007.

21. Paine, Thomas. *The Age of Reason*. New York: Cosimo, 2005.

22. *Common Sense*. New York: Dover Publications Inc., 1997.

23. *The Rights of Man*. New York: Dover Publications Inc., 1999.

24. *The Thomas Paine Reader*. Edited by Michael Foot and Isaac Kramnick. London: Penguin, 1987.

25. *The Writings of Thomas Paine*. Edited by Moncure Daniel Conway. New York: G.P. Putnam and Sons, 1894. Accessed December 8, 2014, http://oll.libertyfund.org/titles/1083.

26. Philip, Mark. Introduction to *Rights of Man, Common Sense, and Other Political Writings*, by Thomas Paine. Oxford: Oxford University Press. 2008.

27. Rosenfeld, Sophia. *Common Sense: A Political History*. Cambridge, MA: Harvard University Press, 2011.

28. Virilio, Paul. *The Information Bomb.* Translated by Chris Turner. London: Verso, 2005.

29. Wraight, Christopher D. *Rousseau's* The Social Contract*: A Reader's Guide*. London and New York: Continuum, 2008.

原书作者简介

托马斯·潘恩 1737 年出生在英国，在穷困而充满宗教色彩的家境中长大，几乎未接受过正规教育。1774 年，潘恩在伦敦认识了伟大的北美殖民地政治家富兰克林，人生轨迹就此发生改变。在富兰克林的帮助下，潘恩移民到北美殖民地。潘恩的政治作品如《常识》等激发了北美民众的不满，并致引发美国独立革命。潘恩一生致力于提升社会道德与公正，1809 年在纽约新罗谢尔去世，享年 72 岁。

本书作者简介

伊恩·杰克逊，英国兰卡斯特大学政治、哲学与宗教系博士生，研究方向是新媒体在思想传播中的作用。

世界名著中的批判性思维

《世界思想宝库钥匙丛书》致力于深入浅出地阐释全世界著名思想家的观点，不论是谁、在何处都能了解到，从而推进批判性思维发展。

《世界思想宝库钥匙丛书》与世界顶尖大学的一流学者合作，为一系列学科中最有影响的著作推出新的分析文本，介绍其观点和影响。在这一不断扩展的系列中，每种选入的著作都代表了历经时间考验的思想典范。通过为这些著作提供必要背景、揭示原作者的学术渊源以及说明这些著作所产生的影响，本系列图书希望让读者以新视角看待这些划时代的经典之作。读者应学会思考、运用并挑战这些著作中的观点，而不是简单接受它们。

ABOUT THE AUTHOR OF THE ORIGINAL WORK

Born in Britain in 1737, **Thomas Paine** had a humble, religious upbringing and very little formal education. The course of his life turned in 1774, when he met the great American statesman Benjamin Franklin in London. With Franklin's help, Paine emigrated to the American colonies, where his political writings such as *Common Sense* contributed to the discontent that resulted in the American Revolution. Paine maintained his stubborn commitment to morality and social justice until his death in 1809 in New Rochelle, New York at the age of 72.

ABOUT THE AUTHOR OF THE ANALYSIS

Ian Jackson is a PhD student in the Politics, Philosophy and Religion department at Lancaster University. He is interested in the role new media plays in the dissemination of ideas.

ABOUT MACAT
GREAT WORKS FOR CRITICAL THINKING

Macat is focused on making the ideas of the world's great thinkers accessible and comprehensible to everybody, everywhere, in ways that promote the development of enhanced critical thinking skills.

It works with leading academics from the world's top universities to produce new analyses that focus on the ideas and the impact of the most influential works ever written across a wide variety of academic disciplines. Each of the works that sit at the heart of its growing library is an enduring example of great thinking. But by setting them in context — and looking at the influences that shaped their authors, as well as the responses they provoked — Macat encourages readers to look at these classics and game-changers with fresh eyes. Readers learn to think, engage and challenge their ideas, rather than simply accepting them.

批判性思维与《常识》

首要批判性思维技巧：理性化思维

次要批判性思维技巧：创造性思维

托马斯·潘恩的《常识》（1776）是历史上最具爆炸性和革命性的书籍之一，具有不可动摇的地位。《常识》是美国独立革命之初出版的一本薄薄的小宣传册，被北美殖民地民众广泛阅读，至今还是美国历史上经久不衰的畅销书。

《常识》积极为北美独立并建立民主政府而鼓与呼。几乎可以说该书对改变世界面貌所产生的影响要大于其他任何书籍。潘恩的这本小册子也是一本批判性思维的高级培训手册，向人们展示了通过文学技巧和热情可以加强论点的逻辑建构。与其说潘恩可能是一个著名的论点建构者，还不如说他更是一个文论家，但是《常识》把良性推理和激烈论辩的最佳要素结合起来。从系统论证政府的起源，到系统批判君主制，再到系统论证美国独立后建立民主政府的可行性，潘恩有条不紊地列出了一系列有说服力的理由，号召北美人民为独立和建立新政府而战。实际上，正如书名所示，这样做完全是一种"常识"。

CRITICAL THINKING AND *COMMON SENSE*

- Primary critical thinking skill: REASONING
- Secondary critical thinking skill: CREATIVE THINKING

Thomas Paine's 1776 *Common Sense* has secured an unshakeable place as one of history's most explosive and revolutionary books. A slim pamphlet published at the beginning of the American Revolution, it was so widely read that it remains the all-time best selling book in US history.

An impassioned argument for American independence and for democratic government, *Common Sense* can claim to have helped change the face of the world more than almost any other book. But Paine's pamphlet is also a masterclass in critical thinking, demonstrating how the reasoned construction of arguments can be reinforced by literary skill and passion. Paine is perhaps more famous as a stylist than as a constructor of arguments, but *Common Sense* marries the best elements of good reasoning to its polemic. Moving systematically from the origins of government, through a criticism of monarchy, and on to the possibilities for future democratic government in an independent America, Paine neatly lays out a series of persuasive reasons to fight for independence and a new form of government. Indeed, as the pamphlet's title suggested, to do so was nothing more than "common sense."

《世界思想宝库钥匙丛书》简介

《世界思想宝库钥匙丛书》致力于为一系列在各领域产生重大影响的人文社科类经典著作提供独特的学术探讨。每一本读物都不仅仅是原经典著作的内容摘要，而是介绍并深入研究原经典著作的学术渊源、主要观点和历史影响。这一丛书的目的是提供一套学习资料，以促进读者掌握批判性思维，从而更全面、深刻地去理解重要思想。

每一本读物分为 3 个部分：学术渊源、学术思想和学术影响，每个部分下有 4 个小节。这些章节旨在从各个方面研究原经典著作及其反响。

由于独特的体例，每一本读物不但易于阅读，而且另有一项优点：所有读物的编排体例相同，读者在进行某个知识层面的调查或研究时可交叉参阅多本该丛书中的相关读物，从而开启跨领域研究的路径。

为了方便阅读，每本读物最后还列出了术语表和人名表（在书中则以星号 * 标记），此外还有参考文献。

《世界思想宝库钥匙丛书》与剑桥大学合作，理清了批判性思维的要点，即如何通过 6 种技能来进行有效思考。其中 3 种技能让我们能够理解问题，另 3 种技能让我们有能力解决问题。这 6 种技能合称为"批判性思维 PACIER 模式"，它们是：

分析：了解如何建立一个观点；
评估：研究一个观点的优点和缺点；
阐释：对意义所产生的问题加以理解；
创造性思维：提出新的见解，发现新的联系；
解决问题：提出切实有效的解决办法；
理性化思维：创建有说服力的观点。

THE MACAT LIBRARY

The Macat Library is a series of unique academic explorations of seminal works in the humanities and social sciences — books and papers that have had a significant and widely recognised impact on their disciplines. It has been created to serve as much more than just a summary of what lies between the covers of a great book. It illuminates and explores the influences on, ideas of, and impact of that book. Our goal is to offer a learning resource that encourages critical thinking and fosters a better, deeper understanding of important ideas.

Each publication is divided into three Sections: Influences, Ideas, and Impact. Each Section has four Modules. These explore every important facet of the work, and the responses to it.

This Section-Module structure makes a Macat Library book easy to use, but it has another important feature. Because each Macat book is written to the same format, it is possible (and encouraged!) to cross-reference multiple Macat books along the same lines of inquiry or research. This allows the reader to open up interesting interdisciplinary pathways.

To further aid your reading, lists of glossary terms and people mentioned are included at the end of this book (these are indicated by an asterisk [*] throughout) — as well as a list of works cited.

Macat has worked with the University of Cambridge to identify the elements of critical thinking and understand the ways in which six different skills combine to enable effective thinking.

Three allow us to fully understand a problem; three more give us the tools to solve it. Together, these six skills make up the PACIER model of critical thinking. They are:

ANALYSIS — understanding how an argument is built
EVALUATION — exploring the strengths and weaknesses of an argument
INTERPRETATION — understanding issues of meaning
CREATIVE THINKING — coming up with new ideas and fresh connections
PROBLEM-SOLVING — producing strong solutions
REASONING — creating strong arguments

"《世界思想宝库钥匙丛书》提供了独一无二的跨学科学习和研究工具。它介绍那些革新了各自学科研究的经典著作，还邀请全世界一流专家和教育机构进行严谨的分析，为每位读者打开世界顶级教育的大门。"

—— 安德烈亚斯·施莱歇尔，
经济合作与发展组织教育与技能司司长

"《世界思想宝库钥匙丛书》直面大学教育的巨大挑战……他们组建了一支精干而活跃的学者队伍，来推出在研究广度上颇具新意的教学材料。"

—— 布罗尔斯教授、勋爵，剑桥大学前校长

"《世界思想宝库钥匙丛书》的愿景令人赞叹。它通过分析和阐释那些曾深刻影响人类思想以及社会、经济发展的经典文本，提供了新的学习方法。它推动批判性思维，这对于任何社会和经济体来说都是至关重要的。这就是未来的学习方法。"

—— 查尔斯·克拉克阁下，英国前教育大臣

"对于那些影响了各自领域的著作，《世界思想宝库钥匙丛书》能让人们立即了解到围绕那些著作展开的评论性言论，这让该系列图书成为在这些领域从事研究的师生们不可或缺的资源。"

—— 威廉·特朗佐教授，加利福尼亚大学圣地亚哥分校

"Macat offers an amazing first-of-its-kind tool for interdisciplinary learning and research. Its focus on works that transformed their disciplines and its rigorous approach, drawing on the world's leading experts and educational institutions, opens up a world-class education to anyone."

—— Andreas Schleicher, Director for Education and Skills, Organisation for Economic Co-operation and Development

"Macat is taking on some of the major challenges in university education... They have drawn together a strong team of active academics who are producing teaching materials that are novel in the breadth of their approach."

—— Prof Lord Broers, former Vice-Chancellor of the University of Cambridge

"The Macat vision is exceptionally exciting. It focuses upon new modes of learning which analyse and explain seminal texts which have profoundly influenced world thinking and so social and economic development. It promotes the kind of critical thinking which is essential for any society and economy. This is the learning of the future."

—— Rt Hon Charles Clarke, former UK Secretary of State for Education

"The Macat analyses provide immediate access to the critical conversation surrounding the books that have shaped their respective discipline, which will make them an invaluable resource to all of those, students and teachers, working in the field."

—— Prof William Tronzo, University of California at San Diego

✪ The Macat Library
世界思想宝库钥匙丛书

TITLE	中文书名	类别
An Analysis of Arjun Appadurai's *Modernity at Large: Cultural Dimensions of Globalization*	解析阿尔君·阿帕杜莱《消失的现代性：全球化的文化维度》	人类学
An Analysis of Claude Lévi-Strauss's *Structural Anthropology*	解析克劳德·列维-斯特劳斯《结构人类学》	人类学
An Analysis of Marcel Mauss's *The Gift*	解析马塞尔·莫斯《礼物》	人类学
An Analysis of Jared M. Diamond's *Guns, Germs, and Steel: The Fate of Human Societies*	解析贾雷德·M.戴蒙德《枪炮、病菌与钢铁：人类社会的命运》	人类学
An Analysis of Clifford Geertz's *The Interpretation of Cultures*	解析克利福德·格尔茨《文化的解释》	人类学
An Analysis of Philippe Ariès's *Centuries of Childhood: A Social History of Family Life*	解析菲力浦·阿利埃斯《儿童的世纪：旧制度下的儿童和家庭生活》	人类学
An Analysis of W. Chan Kim & Renée Mauborgne's *Blue Ocean Strategy*	解析金伟灿/勒妮·莫博涅《蓝海战略》	商业
An Analysis of John P. Kotter's *Leading Change*	解析约翰·P.科特《领导变革》	商业
An Analysis of Michael E. Porter's *Competitive Strategy: Techniques for Analyzing Industries and Competitors*	解析迈克尔·E.波特《竞争战略：分析产业和竞争对手的技术》	商业
An Analysis of Jean Lave & Etienne Wenger's *Situated Learning: Legitimate Peripheral Participation*	解析琼·莱夫/艾蒂纳·温格《情境学习：合法的边缘性参与》	商业
An Analysis of Douglas McGregor's *The Human Side of Enterprise*	解析道格拉斯·麦格雷戈《企业的人性面》	商业
An Analysis of Milton Friedman's *Capitalism and Freedom*	解析米尔顿·弗里德曼《资本主义与自由》	商业
An Analysis of Ludwig von Mises's *The Theory of Money and Credit*	解析路德维希·冯·米塞斯《货币和信用理论》	经济学
An Analysis of Adam Smith's *The Wealth of Nations*	解析亚当·斯密《国富论》	经济学
An Analysis of Thomas Piketty's *Capital in the Twenty-First Century*	解析托马斯·皮凯蒂《21世纪资本论》	经济学
An Analysis of Nassim Nicholas Taleb's *The Black Swan: The Impact of the Highly Improbable*	解析纳西姆·尼古拉斯·塔勒布《黑天鹅：如何应对不可预知的未来》	经济学
An Analysis of Ha-Joon Chang's *Kicking Away the Ladder*	解析张夏准《富国陷阱：发达国家为何踢开梯子》	经济学
An Analysis of Thomas Robert Malthus's *An Essay on the Principle of Population*	解析托马斯·罗伯特·马尔萨斯《人口论》	经济学

An Analysis of John Maynard Keynes's *The General Theory of Employment, Interest and Money*	解析约翰·梅纳德·凯恩斯《就业、利息和货币通论》	经济学
An Analysis of Milton Friedman's *The Role of Monetary Policy*	解析米尔顿·弗里德曼《货币政策的作用》	经济学
An Analysis of Burton G. Malkiel's *A Random Walk Down Wall Street*	解析伯顿·G.马尔基尔《漫步华尔街》	经济学
An Analysis of Friedrich A. Hayek's *The Road to Serfdom*	解析弗里德里希·A.哈耶克《通往奴役之路》	经济学
An Analysis of Charles P. Kindleberger's *Manias, Panics, and Crashes: A History of Financial Crises*	解析查尔斯·P.金德尔伯格《疯狂、惊恐和崩溃：金融危机史》	经济学
An Analysis of Amartya Sen's *Development as Freedom*	解析阿马蒂亚·森《以自由看待发展》	经济学
An Analysis of Rachel Carson's *Silent Spring*	解析蕾切尔·卡森《寂静的春天》	地理学
An Analysis of Charles Darwin's *On the Origin of Species: by Means of Natural Selection, or The Preservation of Favoured Races in the Struggle for Life*	解析查尔斯·达尔文《物种起源》	地理学
An Analysis of World Commission on Environment and Development's *The Brundtland Report: Our Common Future*	解析世界环境与发展委员会《布伦特兰报告：我们共同的未来》	地理学
An Analysis of James E. Lovelock's *Gaia: A New Look at Life on Earth*	解析詹姆斯·E.拉伍洛克《盖娅：地球生命的新视野》	地理学
An Analysis of Paul Kennedy's *The Rise and Fall of the Great Powers: Economic Change and Military Conflict from 1500–2000*	解析保罗·肯尼迪《大国的兴衰：1500—2000年的经济变革与军事冲突》	历史
An Analysis of Janet L. Abu-Lughod's *Before European Hegemony: The World System A. D. 1250–1350*	解析珍妮特·L.阿布–卢格霍德《欧洲霸权之前：1250—1350年的世界体系》	历史
An Analysis of Alfred W. Crosby's *The Columbian Exchange: Biological and Cultural Consequences of 1492*	解析艾尔弗雷德·W.克罗斯比《哥伦布大交换：1492年以后的生物影响和文化冲击》	历史
An Analysis of Tony Judt's *Postwar: A History of Europe since 1945*	解析托尼·朱特《战后欧洲史》	历史
An Analysis of Richard J. Evans's *In Defence of History*	解析理查德·J.艾文斯《捍卫历史》	历史
An Analysis of Eric Hobsbawm's *The Age of Revolution: Europe 1789–1848*	解析艾瑞克·霍布斯鲍姆《革命的年代：欧洲1789—1848年》	历史

An Analysis of Roland Barthes's *Mythologies*	解析罗兰·巴特《神话学》	文学与批判理论
An Analysis of Simone de Beauvoir's *The Second Sex*	解析西蒙娜·德·波伏娃《第二性》	文学与批判理论
An Analysis of Edward W. Said's *Orientalism*	解析爱德华·W. 萨义德《东方主义》	文学与批判理论
An Analysis of Virginia Woolf's *A Room of One's Own*	解析弗吉尼亚·伍尔芙《一间自己的房间》	文学与批判理论
An Analysis of Judith Butler's *Gender Trouble*	解析朱迪斯·巴特勒《性别麻烦》	文学与批判理论
An Analysis of Ferdinand de Saussure's *Course in General Linguistics*	解析费尔迪南·德·索绪尔《普通语言学教程》	文学与批判理论
An Analysis of Susan Sontag's *On Photography*	解析苏珊·桑塔格《论摄影》	文学与批判理论
An Analysis of Walter Benjamin's *The Work of Art in the Age of Mechanical Reproduction*	解析瓦尔特·本雅明《机械复制时代的艺术作品》	文学与批判理论
An Analysis of W. E. B. Du Bois's *The Souls of Black Folk*	解析 W.E.B. 杜波依斯《黑人的灵魂》	文学与批判理论
An Analysis of Plato's *The Republic*	解析柏拉图《理想国》	哲学
An Analysis of Plato's *Symposium*	解析柏拉图《会饮篇》	哲学
An Analysis of Aristotle's *Metaphysics*	解析亚里士多德《形而上学》	哲学
An Analysis of Aristotle's *Nicomachean Ethics*	解析亚里士多德《尼各马可伦理学》	哲学
An Analysis of Immanuel Kant's *Critique of Pure Reason*	解析伊曼努尔·康德《纯粹理性批判》	哲学
An Analysis of Ludwig Wittgenstein's *Philosophical Investigations*	解析路德维希·维特根斯坦《哲学研究》	哲学
An Analysis of G. W. F. Hegel's *Phenomenology of Spirit*	解析 G. W. F. 黑格尔《精神现象学》	哲学
An Analysis of Baruch Spinoza's *Ethics*	解析巴鲁赫·斯宾诺莎《伦理学》	哲学
An Analysis of Hannah Arendt's *The Human Condition*	解析汉娜·阿伦特《人的境况》	哲学
An Analysis of G. E. M. Anscombe's *Modern Moral Philosophy*	解析 G. E. M. 安斯康姆《现代道德哲学》	哲学
An Analysis of David Hume's *An Enquiry Concerning Human Understanding*	解析大卫·休谟《人类理解研究》	哲学

An Analysis of Søren Kierkegaard's *Fear and Trembling*	解析索伦·克尔凯郭尔《恐惧与战栗》	哲学
An Analysis of René Descartes's *Meditations on First Philosophy*	解析勒内·笛卡尔《第一哲学沉思录》	哲学
An Analysis of Friedrich Nietzsche's *On the Genealogy of Morality*	解析弗里德里希·尼采《论道德的谱系》	哲学
An Analysis of Gilbert Ryle's *The Concept of Mind*	解析吉尔伯特·赖尔《心的概念》	哲学
An Analysis of Thomas Kuhn's *The Structure of Scientific Revolutions*	解析托马斯·库恩《科学革命的结构》	哲学
An Analysis of John Stuart Mill's *Utilitarianism*	解析约翰·斯图亚特·穆勒《功利主义》	哲学
An Analysis of Aristotle's *Politics*	解析亚里士多德《政治学》	政治学
An Analysis of Niccolò Machiavelli's *The Prince*	解析尼科洛·马基雅维利《君主论》	政治学
An Analysis of Karl Marx's *Capital*	解析卡尔·马克思《资本论》	政治学
An Analysis of Benedict Anderson's *Imagined Communities*	解析本尼迪克特·安德森《想象的共同体》	政治学
An Analysis of Samuel P. Huntington's *The Clash of Civilizations and the Remaking of World Order*	解析塞缪尔·P.亨廷顿《文明的冲突与世界秩序的重建》	政治学
An Analysis of Alexis de Tocqueville's *Democracy in America*	解析阿列克西·德·托克维尔《论美国的民主》	政治学
An Analysis of John A. Hobson's *Imperialism: A Study*	解析约翰·A.霍布森《帝国主义》	政治学
An Analysis of Thomas Paine's *Common Sense*	解析托马斯·潘恩《常识》	政治学
An Analysis of John Rawls's *A Theory of Justice*	解析约翰·罗尔斯《正义论》	政治学
An Analysis of Francis Fukuyama's *The End of History and the Last Man*	解析弗朗西斯·福山《历史的终结与最后的人》	政治学
An Analysis of John Locke's *Two Treatises of Government*	解析约翰·洛克《政府论》	政治学
An Analysis of Sun Tzu's *The Art of War*	解析孙武《孙子兵法》	政治学
An Analysis of Henry Kissinger's *World Order: Reflections on the Character of Nations and the Course of History*	解析亨利·基辛格《世界秩序》	政治学
An Analysis of Jean-Jacques Rousseau's *The Social Contract*	解析让-雅克·卢梭《社会契约论》	政治学

An Analysis of Odd Arne Westad's *The Global Cold War: Third World Interventions and the Making of Our Times*	解析文安立《全球冷战：美苏对第三世界的干涉与当代世界的形成》	政治学
An Analysis of Sigmund Freud's *The Interpretation of Dreams*	解析西格蒙德·弗洛伊德《梦的解析》	心理学
An Analysis of William James' *The Principles of Psychology*	解析威廉·詹姆斯《心理学原理》	心理学
An Analysis of Philip Zimbardo's *The Lucifer Effect*	解析菲利普·津巴多《路西法效应》	心理学
An Analysis of Leon Festinger's *A Theory of Cognitive Dissonance*	解析利昂·费斯汀格《认知失调论》	心理学
An Analysis of Richard H. Thaler & Cass R. Sunstein's *Nudge: Improving Decisions about Health, Wealth, and Happiness*	解析理查德·H.泰勒/卡斯·R.桑斯坦《助推：如何做出有关健康、财富和幸福的更优决策》	心理学
An Analysis of Gordon Allport's *The Nature of Prejudice*	解析高尔登·奥尔波特《偏见的本质》	心理学
An Analysis of Steven Pinker's *The Better Angels of Our Nature: Why Violence Has Declined*	解析斯蒂芬·平克《人性中的善良天使：暴力为什么会减少》	心理学
An Analysis of Stanley Milgram's *Obedience to Authority*	解析斯坦利·米尔格拉姆《对权威的服从》	心理学
An Analysis of Betty Friedan's *The Feminine Mystique*	解析贝蒂·弗里丹《女性的奥秘》	心理学
An Analysis of David Riesman's *The Lonely Crowd: A Study of the Changing American Character*	解析大卫·理斯曼《孤独的人群：美国人社会性格演变之研究》	社会学
An Analysis of Franz Boas's *Race, Language and Culture*	解析弗朗兹·博厄斯《种族、语言与文化》	社会学
An Analysis of Pierre Bourdieu's *Outline of a Theory of Practice*	解析皮埃尔·布尔迪厄《实践理论大纲》	社会学
An Analysis of Max Weber's *The Protestant Ethic and the Spirit of Capitalism*	解析马克斯·韦伯《新教伦理与资本主义精神》	社会学
An Analysis of Jane Jacobs's *The Death and Life of Great American Cities*	解析简·雅各布斯《美国大城市的死与生》	社会学
An Analysis of C. Wright Mills's *The Sociological Imagination*	解析C.赖特·米尔斯《社会学的想象力》	社会学
An Analysis of Robert E. Lucas Jr.'s *Why Doesn't Capital Flow from Rich to Poor Countries?*	解析小罗伯特·E.卢卡斯《为何资本不从富国流向穷国？》	社会学

An Analysis of Émile Durkheim's *On Suicide*	解析埃米尔·迪尔凯姆《自杀论》	社会学
An Analysis of Eric Hoffer's *The True Believer: Thoughts on the Nature of Mass Movements*	解析埃里克·霍弗《狂热分子：群众运动圣经》	社会学
An Analysis of Jared M. Diamond's *Collapse: How Societies Choose to Fail or Survive*	解析贾雷德·M.戴蒙德《大崩溃：社会如何选择兴亡》	社会学
An Analysis of Michel Foucault's *The History of Sexuality Vol. 1: The Will to Knowledge*	解析米歇尔·福柯《性史（第一卷）：求知意志》	社会学
An Analysis of Michel Foucault's *Discipline and Punish*	解析米歇尔·福柯《规训与惩罚》	社会学
An Analysis of Richard Dawkins's *The Selfish Gene*	解析理查德·道金斯《自私的基因》	社会学
An Analysis of Antonio Gramsci's *Prison Notebooks*	解析安东尼奥·葛兰西《狱中札记》	社会学
An Analysis of Augustine's *Confessions*	解析奥古斯丁《忏悔录》	神学
An Analysis of C. S. Lewis's *The Abolition of Man*	解析 C. S. 路易斯《人之废》	神学

图书在版编目（CIP）数据

解析托马斯·潘恩《常识》: 汉、英 / 伊恩·杰克逊（Ian Jackson）著；
杨元刚译. —上海：上海外语教育出版社，2020
（世界思想宝库钥匙丛书）
ISBN 978-7-5446-6539-1

Ⅰ.①解… Ⅱ.①伊… ②杨… Ⅲ.①政治思想史－美国－近代 Ⅳ.①D097.124

中国版本图书馆CIP数据核字（2020）第177595号

This Chinese-English bilingual edition of *An Analysis of Thomas Paine's* Common Sense is
published by arrangement with MACAT International Limited.
Licensed for sale throughout the world.

本书汉英双语版由Macat国际有限公司授权上海外语教育出版社有限公司出版。
供在全世界范围内发行、销售。

图字：09－2018－549

出版发行：**上海外语教育出版社**
　　　　　（上海外国语大学内）　邮编：200083
电　　话：021-65425300（总机）
电子邮箱：bookinfo@sflep.com.cn
网　　址：http://www.sflep.com
责任编辑：张　宏

印　　刷：上海叶大印务发展有限公司
开　　本：890×1240　1/32　印张 5.125　字数 106千字
版　　次：2021 年 2 月第 1 版　　2021 年 2 月第 1 次印刷

书　　号：ISBN 978-7-5446-6539-1
定　　价：30.00 元
　　　　本版图书如有印装质量问题，可向本社调换
　　　　质量服务热线：4008-213-263　电子邮箱：editorial@sflep.com